BullyProof Yourself & Your Kids

Don't Believe A Bully!

The Little Book of Peaceful Power

Brenda Miller

BALBOA.PRESS

A DIVISION OF HAY HOUSE

Balboa Press books may be ordered through booksellers or by contacting:

Balboa Press
A Division of Hay House
1663 Liberty Drive
Bloomington, IN 47403
www.balboapress.com
844-682-1282

Because of the dynamic nature of the Internet, any web addresses or links contained in this book may have changed since publication and may no longer be valid. The views expressed in this work are solely those of the author and do not necessarily reflect the views of the publisher, and the publisher hereby disclaims any responsibility for them.

The author of this book does not dispense medical advice or prescribe the use of any technique as a form of treatment for physical, emotional, or medical problems without the advice of a physician, either directly or indirectly. The intent of the author is only to offer information of a general nature to help you in your quest for emotional and spiritual well-being. In the event you use any of the information in this book for yourself, which is your constitutional right, the author and the publisher assume no responsibility for your actions.

Any people depicted in stock imagery provided by Getty Images are models, and such images are being used for illustrative purposes only. Certain stock imagery © Getty Images.

Print information available on the last page.

ISBN: 978-1-9822-7968-4 (sc)
ISBN: 978-1-9822-7969-1 (e)

Balboa Press rev. date: 02/09/2022

The little book of peaceful power.

ACKNOWLEDGEMENTS

Thank you to everyone who has supported, produced and made this work available to help human beings regain what would seem to be a basic human right—peaceful sovereignty over our own lives.

The little book of peaceful power.

The little book of peaceful power.

Dedication

This book is dedicated to everyone who has ever been
bullied, and to every bully who wants to stop.

The little book of peaceful power.

CONTENTS

The little book of peaceful power.

The little book of peaceful power.

CHAPTER 1

You Are Not Powerless

"When people hurt you over and over,
think of them like sandpaper.
They may scratch and hurt you a bit,
but in the end, you end up polished
and they end up useless."
-Chris Colfer

This book is to radically change your experience of a bully.

It's to help you get the target off of your back as a victim.

It's to help educate you so you can keep bully tactics on your radar and recognize them the moment they appear.

It's to help you find peace no matter how long a bully has been disrupting your life.

It's to help you stop bullying yourself and others.

This book is to help you
meet and defeat a bully.

If there is a bully in your life right now, or has been in the past, you already know that it can be earth shattering when they invade your family, the workplace, or your social circles. They make you feel powerless. You're not. You have something inside of you that is stronger than you think—let's find that.

The little book of peaceful power.

1

Inner Power

If there are no heroes to save you,
then you be the hero.
-Denpa kyoshi

What exists inside of us is a connection to the same pure intelligence that operates nature in all its glory and perfection. When we revert to our own True Nature, we are like a kid, playful, wise, belly laughing, inclusive, and genuine. How we know that to be true, is that when we are in those states, we *feel* natural. In these states we are coherent and when we're coherent, we're joyfully harmless.

Other names for our True Nature, which is the ultimate in the human experience of mental and emotional balance are:

- Original Nature
- Essential Nature
- True Self
- Natural Self
- The Deeper I (As taught by Eckhart Tolle, spiritual teacher)
- Creation
- Isness (As taught by Mooji, spiritual teacher)
- Zero Point Field
- Source
- Divine or Pure Intelligence
- Buddha Nature
- Christ Consciousness
- Your name for who you celebrate or worship as having created everything.

Who Can Use This Book?

Wrong is wrong even if everyone is doing it.
Right is right even if no one is doing it.
-*St. Augustine*

The book will be helpful for:

- Parents who have children who are being bullied
- Adults who have been or are being bullied
- Parenting groups
- Schools
- Organizations that work to prevent bullying
- Bullies
- Victims

How To Use This Book?

Knowing what's right doesn't mean much
unless you do what's right.
-Theodore Roosevelt

For Parents

If you are going to help a child with bullying, it will be necessary to do each of the exercises yourself, using your experience with a bully (or someone who is abusive or overly critical towards you) before you will be able to help your child. Once you experience relief using the exercises you will be able to confidently share them with your child.

After reading the book you are invited to:

For Schools

Contact me through www.thekidcode.ca for a free book for all teachers and admin, and a Zoom training for you, your students and their parents.

For the Workplace

Book a Staff Training Session on my website.

BullyProof Buddies

One person can make a difference,
and everyone should try.
-John F. Kennedy

A BullyProof buddy can support and help us understand and use these strategies. The actual inner work (the questions we ask to find answers inside of ourselves) can only be done by us. At the same time, the findings can be shared with a friend who often discovers other beliefs—that we can also relate to and release. That helps us take our work deeper and as a result, gain more freedom.

Powering Out of Chaos Into Coherence

"I constantly felt confused, helpless
and afraid—with nowhere to turn."
-Anonymous

We need to be coherent so we can take clear actions to get ourselves out of the bully's bulls eye, out of chaos, and out of victimhood.

If we're in bully-mode we need to dissolve the drivers in us that are creating that state because being a bully is painful.

A simple definition of coherence is: orderly, harmonious, and makes sense. We feel best in this state. We never truly feel good when we're in bully- or victim-mode. When we are coherent, we are capable of intelligent perception, speech, thought and actions.

A bully is incapable of intelligence when they are bullying. We become incoherent and more and more chaotic when we are about to bully ourselves or others.

Coherence is the state of being where we are able to:

- feel refreshed and invigorated
- feel relaxed, even with deadlines
- feel all of our natural states: compassion, joyful, inclusive, belly laughing, playful, loving, etc.
- experience clear thinking and a clear mind.

Coherence is our natural state. That's why we are brought back to it with any strategy we use to dissolve stress. Each of the strategies in this book are designed to do that.

Why I Wrote This Book?

No one heals himself by wounding another.
-St. Ambrose

There were two of them.

He was mad—backing away, spewing hatred, "I've got a gun you know," he growled. I froze. I didn't know what to say or do. Was he going to get his gun? What was happening here?

It was a long time before I felt comfortable going to sleep.

It wasn't unusual for him to aggressively, verbally attack, or for her to, either. They'd both been doing it for so long we thought it was normal. But this time, when he said, "I've got a gun, you know," it went too far. Yes, I did know. I didn't think it would become a prop in his bullying tactics. I was wrong.

Sometimes we put up with something for a long time for a lot of reasons that aren't apparent to us. Abuse may be familiar but that doesn't make it normal.

First, I wanted to lash out at them—and did, much to my dismay. I acted out against them on purpose in retaliation. Then I wanted to understand because lashing out didn't feel good or right.

In addition to that experience, I spent some of my formative years hiding in a cupboard from a bully. That sent me out into the world in a stressed-out state that turned out to be a gift because it inspired me to find out how to dissolve stress—before it detonates.

After the 'I have a gun' situation, I set out to learn everything I could about bullies. This book and a career in teaching conscious conflict resolution is the result. I'm sharing my story because the tide slowly turned and the bullies took themselves out of my life. If we ever happen to meet, they either stay on the sidelines or attempt politeness.

I watched over several months' time, as I did each of the exercises I discovered or created and he faded out of my existence and at the same time my existence became more and more peaceful. She stopped bullying and hasn't done it since.

I was not powerless.

If we do enough of the type of work that's in this book, we begin to have compassion for the bully because bullies are not bad people, they are people with bad behaviors.

I have witnessed the dramatic change in a person's inner state firsthand in classes all over the world when they do this type of inner work. The most notable was a man in my class who announced he would always hate his mother because she tried to kill him. After we did the work, similar to the work in this book, he said he felt love for her. That's because he reached his True Nature. There is never a good reason for us to suffer when someone else has hurt us.

I wanted to feel peaceful and not act out against others, no matter what was going on in my life.

"Why Bother?

Because right now there is   someone

Out there with

A wound

                    In the exact shape

                    Of your words."

                    -Sean Thomas Dougherty

Bullies Are Teachers (Mean One's, But Still Teachers)

I don't feel like I can be forgiven for bullying other people. I can't forgive myself. Don't bully. If you are a bully, get help to stop it now. You'll regret it if you don't.
-Anonymous

If we *use a strategy with every upset*/challenge/trouble that appears with a bully, we gain insight into ourselves and them, and we can uncover why we have bullies in our lives—and change that.

The paradox is that by *using* all incidents with them, we slowly become inaccessible to them.

Bullies have been among my best teachers. This is what I learned.

- Abuse is not normal or natural.
- I was unconsciously attracting a bully's attention.
- I can get the target off of my back with a little willingness and some mental elbow grease.
- When I saw the bullies after doing these exercises, my responses to them were less intense and so were their bullying behaviors.
- Bullies showed me that I was stuck in victimhood. Using the strategies when I felt like a victim moved me out of that horrible, helpless feeling.
- Bullies, who seemed to rob me of my self-esteem, paradoxically prodded me into finding it. In this way, if you use strategies to uncover the lessons, you will become empowered.

These are good things to know.

Stress is Optional

Even the darkest night will end
and the sun will rise again.
-Victor Hugo

Stress for more than a few minutes is optional. How we can prove that to be true for ourselves is to use a strategy to self-regulate back to our calm nature *every time an upset occurs*—even when the upset arises during an encounter with a bully.

My dad once said to me, "There is no good reason to be upset." Turns out that he's right, as hard as it is to understand—no matter what's going on, being upset will not help it so there is no good reason to be upset. We can catalyze into practical and right action easier, without being upset.

So, if you are being bullied, keep it as the bully's problem since they are the one with the bully behavior. Don't give them the power—don't allow them to affect your world. The only way I know how to do that IS to use a strategy that returns me to my peaceful nature and dissolve beliefs that attract them.

As mentioned earlier and worth repeating—how do we know that our nature is peaceful and calm? When we're in those states, we *feel* natural. When we're in a negative or upset state, we don't feel natural and to me that's proof that a negative state is not our natural state.

If a bully is in our lives, and we are (as would be expected) terribly reactive to it, we need strategies to de-stress quickly.

Why should we suffer just because a bully is being a bully? Why should we feel bad if we've been bullied?

I offer you these ideas so that you can begin to remember to self-regulate when a bully appears.

While nobody has the right to dump on us, they're going to, so it's helpful to have ways to calm ourselves down when they do.

To be clear, the *arising* of stress or an upset is not optional because whatever we learned and experienced as children is stored in memory and being called on to navigate current situations. All upsetting thoughts and emotions we have in any moment are regurgitated from painful childhood experiences. That is the main value of looking inside to see what's causing us to feel upset rather than blaming another person. Other people did not reach in an install our anger, victimhood, etc. That's easy to understand. But it's almost impossible to understand that what we're feeling inside of us during an upset *is because of what is stored inside of us*. This should be good news. It means others (bullies) don't have the power to turn our upsetting emotions on. Our emotional upsets are happening inside of us, so that's where we can go to dissolve them. They can be catalyzed by others and situations, but everything we feel inside is ours to work out. And, it's important to remember that we can't do any differently than we do until we have new knowledge and self-awareness.

One night when someone was bullying me, I didn't react, I stayed calm. Why? The reactive past wasn't activated. My True Nature was activated. I walked up to him and put my arms around him and his upset dissolved. On another occasion I reacted to the bully and belittled him. I noticed that was fuel for the fire. The first way of responding did more good than the second way of reacting.

Other names for our reactive past are:

- Identified—an example is, when I'm identified as a victim, I will explain it to you rationally or demand you listen and agree. Identification means I have a stake in upholding an idea about myself (that isn't true). I may be experiencing bullying sometimes, but a victim is not who I am. How we can know this to be true is that if all of a sudden no one harms me anymore, how can I be a victim? If victimhood can disappear, how can it be me? When I am identified as a victim, I am believing, thinking, speaking and acting as though I am a victim.

- Attachment—clinging to an idea or an identity as though identity is a truth rather than a learned behavior. Many of us attach to feeling like a victim to get help or in the hopes that someone won't hurt us. We can skip the victim step and jump right to asking for help or removing ourselves from situations where people are determined to hurt us.
- Emotional Memory—when we're little and experience a trauma, the memory and emotions store in our unconscious mind. When we grow up and meet certain situations that unconsciously remind us of that initial trauma, the upsetting emotions rise up all over again to try to help us avoid that painful situation. Being upset has never truly helped us solve a situation.
- Ego—adopted ideas and formed patterns that provide us with unsuccessful strategies for success. The part of the ego that is the victim is the part of the ego that protects this painful way of being in the world. The ego wants us to stay victims. Our Essential Nature wants us to dissolve it.

We don't need any of those states anymore; we have our True Nature. Understanding this is empowering.

CHAPTER 2

BullyProof Basics

I would rather be a little nobody than an evil somebody.
-Abraham Lincoln

Record & Report

Bullies thrive on secrecy—yours.
Tell someone who can help.
-Anonymous

Record all bullying events including details as honestly as you can:

- Date, time, location.
- Who was there and how to contact them.
- What each person did and said (including you).
- General impressions.
- Outcomes—injuries, etc.

Report this information to an authority or someone *you trust.*

Local & Federal Laws on Bullying

Bullies will try to get away with whatever they can,
regardless of rules or laws. Don't let them.
-Anonymous

Look up the laws about bullying in your area so you're informed about your rights and where to go to ensure you keep them.

A Little Bit of Roughhousing

"Bullying can scar. Don't let it get that far."
-Anonymous

When someone hits, pushes, criticizes, is mean, rude, or demonstrates other nasty behaviors one time or maybe a couple of times, that's not considered bullying. It's not acceptable either, but we're all going to encounter that kind of behavior at some time in our lives. That said, you can use these strategies successfully when those situations occur to help them from becoming bullying.

Bullying is a repeated, threatening, on purpose, power grab with intention to cause harm.

The Bully Defined

The bully is:

> An insecure, gloating, swaggering, quarrelsome, overbearing, unbalanced, and cowardly person...

> ...who seeks out those who doubt themselves,

> ...and then uses force, threats, manipulation, coercion, abuse, badgering, intimidation, embarrassment, and aggression,

> ...to dominate, harm, make fun of, and frighten,

> ...smaller, weaker or handicapped people,

> ...in order to gain a quick but false sense of strength and power.

Except that true power is peaceful and true peace is powerful, and the power the bully gains is destructive, so they never achieve what they hope for.

Examples of people who understand peaceful power are Nelson Mandela, Mother Teresa, Martin Luther King Jr., and Mahatma Gandhi—they each gained and then demonstrated power that was peaceful.

Also, all of us have a bully within. It's the voices or thoughts that push us around, criticize and threaten us—and do the same to others.

We don't need bullies in our lives anymore.

The Victim Defined

No one can make you feel inferior without your consent.
-Eleanor Roosevelt

A victim is an insecure person who feels alone, targeted, helpless, hurt, angry, confused, afraid, attacked, hopeless, ashamed, flawed, withdrawn, and insecure...

...and is likely to experience depression and anxiety, PTSD (post-traumatic stress disorder),

...may dropout or withdraw in order to avoid bullying,

...and, who unknowingly attracts the bully because of hidden insecurities and belief systems unconsciously adopted in childhood (that can be dissolved).

All of us have a victim within. It's the voices or thoughts that convince us we are powerless, helpless and weak.

We don't need to be victims anymore.

The Types of Bullying

I've never known this kind of terrifying fear
from being bullied.
-Anonymous

- Recognizable to all of us is **verbal bullying**—repeated: taunting, gossiping, intimidation, name-calling, attacking: intelligence, appearance, race, religion, gender, culture, and sexuality.
- **Physical bullying**—repeated: pushing, hitting, chasing, grabbing or stealing personal belongings, and unwanted sexual touching.
- **Cyberbullying**—repeated online bullying.
- **Social bullying**—repeated: negative graffiti, mobbing, humiliating others in public (through a speech or written articles, for example).
- **The Inner Bully**—the inner critic that repeatedly threatens you, makes you feel small, ashamed, and powerless.

Covert or Overt

Bullying can be covert (veiled or hidden) or overt (blatant and in the open).

Covert bullies often say things like: "I'm just teasing." "I'm just joking." "Can't you take a joke." Wow, touchy." Gaslighting is also a type of covert bullying where the bully displays unhinged behavior while saying you're the crazy one.

Overt bullying is more apparent—pushy, power-grabbing, and threatening.

To Stop Abuse, Stop Tolerating It.

The funny thing is when you don't let people disrespect you,
they start calling you difficult.
- Onegodquote

Bullying is a painful and serious issue for the victim, the bully, their families and society.

Some public service providers refuse service to people who bully and post signs reinforcing the idea.

Abuse will not be tolerated

Please put this sign up in your home and get permission to put it up in your workplace and schools.

Changing ourselves changes our world; when we do inner work on the bully, the outer world and the people in it change because it is a law that the outer reflects the inner. Said another way, when we change our behavior, those around us change. An easy way to understand this idea is to imagine that when you change your behavior towards a child, the child's behavior changes. For example, if you find the strength to stop hollering at the child, the child's behavior will change—they won't be reacting to hollering.

Notice the inner and outer bully fading out of your experience as you do the work in this book.

We would like to bring understanding to bullying and end it for two reasons:

- Without being told, we know that it doesn't serve us to hurt ourselves or other human beings.
- Bullying can have extreme consequences that are irreversible (death).

Is Your Child Or Someone You Know Being Bullied?

I stayed silent because
I didn't think anyone would believe me.
-Anonymous

There are many signals that could point to someone in your life being bullied. This list arose during my experience with bullies over many years:

- Wanting to be alone, withdrawing.
- Ashamed and not wanting to tell anyone what happened. I kept thinking, "I must be really bad if someone wants to do that to me."
- Heightened startle reflex; unreasonable fear, adrenaline rushes for no good reason.
- Panic attacks.
- Scared of going to sleep in case the bully might come for me.
- Paranoia: projecting fear out onto other things/animals. My paranoia appeared in projecting my fear onto big dogs, even though I'd grown up with and had big dogs during much of my adulthood.
- Having reoccurring nightmares.
- Feeling hopeless and helpless, not knowing where to turn.
- Feeling like a victim, feeling hurt.
- Experiencing trust issues with those whom I could trust.
- Physical ailments: stomach- and headaches (others may experience different physical ailments).
- Making up physical ailments (to get out of participating).
- Feeling intense anger.
- Wanting to hurt the bully. Wishing them harm. Having violent thoughts about them.
- Alternating between intense anger and despair in minutes.

BullyProof Myths

Foolish opinions are not facts

Consider these common myths about bullies:

Myth #1

"Your child (the one being bullied) is overreacting. My child isn't a bully."

- Check it out and see for yourself—you will know if your child is being bullied.
- Many parents don't admit their child is a bully because *they don't want to feel the pain of having a child who is a bully* and they don't want their child's bullying behavior reflecting on them because they think it makes them 'bad' parents.

Myth #2

Kids will be kids.

- If kids demonstrate bullying behaviors, they need to have their behavior corrected for their own benefit and wellbeing, and for the benefit of others. Excusing them is agreeing with bad behavior. We don't want our kids to suffer acting out bad behavior. We know how bad it feels inside of us when we act out!

Myth #3

The bully will outgrow bullying. It's just a stage.

- As Dr. Joe Dispenza, a researcher and international lecturer whose work is based in science, says: "what wires together fires together." The mind gets an idea like bullying makes me tough and wants the experience repeated to confirm it. In this case that means the more we bully and get away with it, the more we'll bully in the future. Don't let your kids or partner get away with it. Nip it in the bud as soon as you see it—for their own sake.

Myth #4

There is nothing to do against a bully—they are too powerful.

- Along with the ideas in this book, bullying organizations, and professionals—there is *powerful help available to you.*

Myth #5

They (the bully) can't help it, they were bullied as a child.

- Anyone can change. It's not easy but it's easier than feeling bad, and a bully does feel bad. When we bully someone, we feel bad, so we know that a bully does too.

Myth #6

You should hit the bully, that will stop them.

- Sometimes it does, but what if the bully is much bigger and stronger than you or is psychologically deranged and hitting them back gets you in more trouble (like severely beaten).
- Even when it turns out to be true that being physical with a bully may be enough to stop them in the moment, what if it starts a war you don't want to be in?

Myth #7

They're just words, they won't cause any damage.

- People who have been seriously verbally bullied have committed suicide.

- While it's true that we are the cause of our own inner feelings based on past experiences, when others abuse us, those bad feelings grow stronger and we cement the upset inside of ourselves and believe them. Then we continually revert to those upsetting ways of being in the world rather than self-regulating back to our calm, peaceful nature.

Myth #8

Your child needs to toughen up.

- It's true that they need to develop some resilience because they will run into bullies—but that doesn't mean making a kid tougher will solve their problems. Helping a child become aware will.

Did You Know?

Boys tend to bully according to group, such as "athlete" versus "non-athlete." Girls tend to bully according to social status, such as "popular" vs. "non-popular."

Source: Karin Lehnardt, September 15, 2015, *57 Interesting Bullying Facts,* September 15, 2015, Updated February 26, 2021, Accessed August 31, 2021. http://facts.randomhistory.com/facts-about-bullying.html

The Usual Anti-Bullying Strategies Are Not Enough

I thought he was going to kill me.
-Anonymous

Our youth are telling a story that needs to be heard so we can change the way we help them.

THIS STUDY SHOWS US THAT WE HAVE TO
REDEFINE HOW WE TEACH KIDS
TO DEAL WITH BULLYING.
WE HAVE TO USE STRATEGIES TO GET THE
TARGET OFF THE VICTIM'S BACK.

The usual strategies are not enough.
Ask anyone who is being bullied.

The Youth Voice Research Project (2010) provides some valuable information and clears up some misconceptions about how to handle bullies.

In the study they asked 11,893 kids from grades five to twelve, in 25 schools across 12 states about being bullied.

Bullying was given four ratings: mild (bullying only bothered them a little bit 46%), moderate (it bothered them quite a bit 36%), severe (the victim had trouble eating, sleeping and enjoying themselves 11%), and very severe (the victim felt unsafe 7%).

Some of their findings go against what kids are traditionally taught about how to deal with bullies:

- Bullying got worse **49% of the time** if <u>the victim hit them or fought them</u> but made it better 31% of the time. 20% of the time fighting back physically made no difference.
- **35% of the time bullying got worse when** <u>the victim walked away</u> and made it better 20% of the time. 45% of the time it made no difference.
- **38% of the time if** <u>the victim told the bully how they felt</u>**, the bullying got worse. 16%** of the time that strategy worked. 46% of the time it made no difference.
- **41% of the time,** <u>telling the bully to stop</u> **made the bullying worse.** It made it better 14% of the time. 46% of the time it made no difference.
- **If** <u>the victim did nothing</u>**, 40% of the time the bullying got worse** and 14% of the time it got better. 47% of the time it made no difference.
- <u>Telling an adult at school</u> **made it worse 29% of the time** and telling the right one made it better 34% of the time. 37% of the time it made no difference.
- <u>Telling an adult at home</u> **made it worse 18% of the time** and better 34% of the time. 48% of the time it made no difference.
- <u>When peers asked the bully to stop</u> **on behalf of the victim, made fun of the victim, or ignored the victim things got worse.**

The Good News

- Peers had an impact in bullying. The study shows that if a **peer spent time with them, talked to them, helped them get away, gave them advice, and helped them tell someone, 44% and up said things got better.** This means victims need to be around their (stable, supportive) peers during the bullying events.
- **"Our students report that asking for and getting emotional support and a sense of connection has helped them the most among all the strategies we compared."**

But it's not enough. We need higher success rates. Again, ask anyone who is being bullied.

"When victims told the adults in school and they ignored it, or gave other negative feedback to the victim, such as telling the victim they should have acted differently, stop tattling, solve the problem themselves, talked about the behavior in class, brought in a speaker, talked to the bully, increased adult supervision for a time, talked to both students together, used punishment for the bully, gave the victim advice, checked with the victim after, and listened to the victim—in all cases their experience of the bully didn't change, the bully's behavior didn't change, or the situation got worse."

"Being told not to tattle had the most negative impact on the students themselves."

Shaming and humiliating kids by telling them not to tattle isn't a solution.

"The actions by self that had some of the most negative impacts (i.e., telling the person to stop, telling the person how I feel, walking away, and pretending it doesn't bother me) were often used by youth and are often recommended to youth. We hope

that the voices of our students can have an effect on the extent to which youth are advised to use these strategies."

Source: Stan Davis, Charisse Nixon, Ph.D. *The Youth Voice Project.* Accessed November 19, 2019

https://njbullying.org/documents/YVPMarch2010.pdf

Bullying Statistics

Teachers said it's just a phase /
When I grow up my children will probably do the same /
Kids just love to tease /
Who'd know it put me underground at seventeen.
-Aaron Solowoniuk; Ben Kowalewicz; Ian D'sa; Jon Gallant

Look up the statistics in your country. It is a problem in every country in the world. It won't change until we change it.

Canadian Statistics

The one time I spoke up, it got worse.
-Anonymous

- At least 1 in 3 adolescent students in Canada have reported being bullied recently.
- Among adult Canadians, 38% of males and 30% of females reported having experienced occasional or frequent bullying during their school years.
- 47% of Canadian parents report having a child victim of bullying.
- Any participation in bullying increases risk of suicidal ideas in youth.
- The rate of discrimination experienced among students who identify as Lesbian, Gay, Bisexual, Trans-identified, Two-Spirited, Queer or Questioning (LGBTQ) is three times higher than heterosexual youth.
- Girls are more likely to be bullied on the Internet than boys.
- 7% of adult Internet users in Canada, age 18 years and older, self-reported having been a victim of cyberbullying at some point in their life.
- The most common form of cyberbullying involved receiving threatening or aggressive e-mails or instant messages, reported by 73% of victims.
- 40% of Canadian workers experience bullying on a weekly basis.

Source: *Canadian Bullying Statistics*. September 28, 2012. Accessed August 19, 2021. https://cihr-irsc.gc.ca/e/45838.html

Bullying Stats in the US

You can hope for it to end, you can wish for it to end, but
in the end, you have to find some way to end it.
-Anonymous

The following is provided by Pacer, the National Bullying Prevention Center:

- 1 in 5 students are bullied (43% in the hallway or stairwell, and 42% in the classroom).
- Prevention programs provided by schools only decreased bullying by up to 25%. (*McCallion & Feder, 2013*)
- 49.8% of tweens (9 to 12 years old) said they experienced bullying at school. (*Patchin & Hinduja, 2020*)
- 37% of people experience cyberbullying (a figure that has more than doubled since 2007). (*Patchin & Hinduja, 2020*)

Source: Pacer's National Bullying Prevention Center, *Bullying Statistics.* Accessed November 26, 2021. https://www.pacer.org/bullying/info/stats.asp

Stats From the UK

When I saw the description of bullying and harassing on a survey
where I worked, that's when I clued in. I was being bullied.
It was so familiar to me I thought that's how life was.
-Anonymous

- 1 in 4 kids—25% of pupils report they're bullied a few times a month.
- Over 16,000 kids miss school due to being bullied.
- Ethnic minorities experience more bullying.
- 55% of bullied kids develop depression.

Source: Aggregate Industries, *9 Shocking Statistics About Bullying in the UK*. Accessed November 19, 2021. https://darkroom.leicestertigers.com/original/2626887647c63a92b4744445d58441e7:7f9e69af2aa9b02297cf54f84deac24f/bullying-facts.pdf

Statistics on Adults Being Bullied

*I went to a human rights commission about being bullied
and they said it was a two year wait
to see if my case was worth accepting.*
-Anonymous

Psychology Today states that a number of studies show that 30% of adults will be bullied (either during their career, or otherwise).

Source: Leah Katz, PhD, Psychology Today, *Adult Bullying Is A Thing, Too.* February 18, 2021, Accessed August 25, 2021 **https://www.psychologytoday.com/ca/blog/here-we-are/202102/adult-bullying-is-thing-too**

UNESCO Institute for Statistics reports that one in three teens are bullied worldwide.

Source: *New Data Reveal That One Out of Three Teens Is Bullied Worldwide.* October 1, 2018. Accessed August 18, 2021, https://en.unesco.org/news/new-data-reveal-one-out-three-teens-bullied-worldwide

Bullying & The Disabled

*Forgiveness is the fragrance that the violet
sheds on the heel that has crushed it.*
-Mark Twain

Eight out of ten children with learning disabilities are bullied.

Anthea Lipsett, *Eight out of 10 disable children bullied, report finds*, The Guardian, June 18, 2007. Accessed January 13, 2022

https://www.theguardian.com/education/2007/jun/18/schools.
children

Cyberbullying Statistics

*The next person you go to hurt / or try to make feel
like dirt / instead of trying to look cool /
feel for the guy you make look a fool*
-Jon Evans

As wonderful as the internet is, cyberbullying is one of the greatest tragedies to come from it.

Media Platforms Where Bullying is Prevalent

If you really want to do something, you'll find a way.
If you don't, you'll find an excuse.
-Jim Rohn

Broadband Search offers these statistics to educate us on where cyberbullying is happening:

- Twitter 9%
- You Tube 10%
- WhatsApp 12%
- Snapchat 31%
- Facebook 37%
- Instagram 42%

Reasons We Get Cyberbullied

If you could get up the courage to begin,
you have the courage to succeed.
-David Viscott

Broadband reports:

- Appearance 61%
- Academic Achievement/Intelligence 25%
- Other 20%
- Race 17%
- Sexuality 15%
- Finances 15%
- Religion 11%

Results of Being Cyberbullied

Anger is an acid that can do more harm to the vessel in which
it is stored than to anything on which is poured.
-Mark Twain

Broadband reported these are the issues that teens feel result from cyberbullying: anxiety, depression, suicidal thoughts, deleted social media profiles or stopped social media, self-harmed, skipped classes, developed eating disorders and began abusing alcohol and drugs.

Signs Someone Is Being Cyberbullied

Strong people stand up for themselves
But the strongest people stand up for others.
-Chris Gardner

- Become shy and withdrawn.
- Be moody, agitated, anxious, or stressed out.
- Act more aggressively towards others.
- Protest more about going to school.
- Get in trouble at school.
- Skip school.
- Experience a dip in academic performance.
- Stop using the computer or other devices that connect to the internet—considered one of the biggest red flags.
- Attempt self-harm or threaten suicide.
- Suddenly start hanging out with a new group of friends.

Source: *All The Latest Cyber Bullying Statistics and What They Mean, What is Cyberbullying, Cyberbullying in 2021.* Accessed November 21, 2021. https://www.broadbandsearch.net/blog/cyber-bullying-statistics

Tactics of the Cyberbully

The test of courage comes
when we are in the minority.
-Ralph W. Sockman

www.Stopbullying.gov offers the following as some of the most common ways to identify a cyberbully:

- Posting comments or rumors about someone online that are mean, hurtful or embarrassing (such as lies or false accusations).
- Threatening to hurt someone or telling them to kill themselves.
- Posting a mean or hurtful picture or video (nude or embarrassing photos that end up on social media due to a breach of trust).
- Pretending to be someone else online in order to solicit or post personal or false information about someone else.
- Posting mean or hateful names, comments, or content about any race, religion, ethnicity, or other personal characteristics (such as being economically challenged) online.
- Creating a mean or hurtful webpage about someone.
- Doxing is a form of online harassment used to exact revenge and to threaten and destroy the privacy of individuals by making their personal information public, including addresses, social security, credit card and phone numbers, link to social media accounts, and other private data so that others can join in the bullying.

Source: *Cyberbullying Tactics* Accessed August 18, 2021. https://www.stopbullying.gov/cyberbullying/cyberbullying-tactics

How to deal with cyberbullying?

Do the right thing. It will gratify some
And astonish the rest.
-Mark Twain

Record, report, get professional help, and do every strategy in this book.

Another Perspective
Blaming The Bully

"A bully is made, not born."
-Dr. Shefali Tsabary

They are a product of their circumstances—a bully becomes one because they were bullied as a child by someone who was bullied and you can trace it backwards and forwards as a generational trauma that needs to stop.

People are living what they learned and that can be changed.

As a course of action, blaming can't change a bully; it feeds them. It does that by confirming that they are the ones in control, in the position of power.

Just as important, blaming the bully is a deflection from the work that would set us free from bullying. We cannot and never will change the other by wishing they'd change or telling them how to change, or stating the obvious: they are bullying, but we can change ourselves, which, paradoxically, changes the way we relate to them. If we do this work and bring awareness to the dynamics between the bully and the victim, we will no longer attract a bully.

We can make these changes by looking at a bully in a whole new way.

Dr. Shefali and Eckhart Tolle Speak on Bullying

The bully is insecure. The victim is insecure.
-Eckhart Tolle & Dr. Shefali Tsabary

This perspective explains bullying in a way most of us have never heard, wouldn't normally consider, and yet it's a way that makes a strange kind of sense.

Eckhart Tolle & Dr. Shefali, respected doctor of clinical psychology, both say that bullies learned they're bad and want to find someone who feels the same way (bad) and bullies them with the hope of riding themselves of the belief and feelings that they themselves *are* bad.

Dr. Shefali says, "If we can 'inoculate' our children or others with the understanding that all of us are good enough just as we are, that takes care of the bully and the victim."

Bullies don't usually pick on people who feel secure (not the second time anyway), and there are exceptions to that rule.

Milton's Secret shows the true resolution lies on the inner level, as taught by Eckhart Tolle. Much of the work in this book is on the inner level.

Eckhart Tolle, Dr. S. Tsabary, *Where Does Bullying Begin?* September 6, 2013. 5:54

https://www.youtube.com/watch?v=uQOcBvJ4kXs

The Importance of Dissolving the Inner Victim & the Bully

You will never reach higher ground
if you are always pushing others down.
-Jeffrey Benjamin

We need to dissolve insecurity inside of ourselves so we are informed by something more stable—our True Nature.

When we bully someone, we're guided by a system inside of ourselves that is causing us pain.

Living from the painful perspective of a bully or a victim is wasting what life offers us—the feeling of being creatively alive and supporting ourselves and others.

What About Confronting a Bully?

When I stood up to them, they came at me harder.
-Anonymous

Always trust your intuition, or if you don't feel like you have good intuition, if you're reading this book, you certainly have common sense, so trust that. Ask the experts, they're only a phone call away. A list of contacts is at the end of the book, but you can look up their phone number now and contact them right away.

While it's possible that a bully will cause physical damage, *it's not likely* according to the statistics. So that means most of them are bluffing to keep some perceived power over a victim. Delfabbro et al. (2006) found that "physical bullying occurred much less frequently than did other types of bullying."

If it is likely that they are going to cause you physical damage, it's important that you get help.

Vetting Violence

Is bullying and violence how they want to be remembered?
-Anonymous

The University of Washington and Indiana says that if a child is exposed to violence between parents, they are more likely to bully.

We know this. Do something about it: get help, do these strategies, and "be your own hero."

Source: Joel Swartz. *Violence in the home leads to higher rates of childhood bullying.* September 12, 2006. Accessed November 13, 2021. https://www.washington.edu/news/2006/09/12/violence-in-the-home-leads-to-higher-rates-of-childhood-bullying/

Bully Buttons

I walked on eggshells around her for most of my life.
It didn't help. I'm done. Get done sooner.
-Anonymous.

There is no good reason to poke a bear—they're grouchy enough as it is. This section is to help you determine your own behavior around a bully to decrease the likelihood of you pushing their buttons. That said, anything from their own unconscious mind can set them off, also. When a person is in bully mode, they are not stable.

To save yourself from aggravating a bully, contemplate some of the things that push a bully's buttons and see if you can notice yourself pulling up into any of the following behaviors around a bully and immediately stop:

- Acting insecure and appearing weak—so stand up straight around them.
- Acting insincere—bullies are just waiting to pounce, and insincerity is as good as an invitation to attack.
- Blaming a bully—that fans the fire.
- Showing defiance or challenging them—bullies are gas lighters trying to point out that you are bad and they are innocent. If you act out, a bully can point their finger at you and that's just what they want—you to be 'the bad one'.
- Exposing them to their face—it can be wise to walk away without calling the bully out, for example, if the bully tells a lie.
- Showing fear.

CHAPTER 3

BullyProof Strategies

Often when you think you're at the end of something,
you're at the beginning of something else.
-Mr. Rogers

Bully Repellant

My self-worth is not linked to your cruel words and actions. My
self-esteem is not affected by your deliberate attempts to destroy my
character. You have no power over me. You will not silence me.
-Marina Cohen

These strategies only take a few minutes and provide two things if you do them until you feel a shift:

1. Immediate relief in the moments of upset because of bullying (that can also be used for the rest of your life and time you encounter abuse or bullying).
2. Ways to dissolve the target on your back, quickly and over time, so bullies aren't attracted to you.

To become BullyProof, you'll have to do all the strategies in the book—some many times. The reason for that is because the beliefs that went on in layers sometimes come off in layers. It's worth it.

Each exercise *is* 'bully repellant'. Don't skip any of the strategies, sit with them instead. "The way out is in," as so wisely stated by Byron Katie, a beloved American spiritual teacher and best-selling author, and

The little book of peaceful power.

Sadhguru, world-renowned mystic and philanthropist. That means we can free ourselves by looking inside of ourselves. When we find out what's in our unconscious mind and let it 'talk' to us, it will show us what beliefs are causing the troubles. All we have to do is ask the right questions, and then listen. That seems simple. It is and it's not.

It's hard to imagine that we have access to the cause of and the cure for (our unknown part in the) bullying right inside of us.

It's not simple because we've been groomed to believe that other people, situations and events are what cause us to feel the way we do (angry, depressed, scared, etc.). That means that others have the power to control our feelings. That makes no sense—that we can each control other people's feelings. What makes more sense is to understand that we alone control our own feelings. That *gives* us the power to control them. If the other controls our feelings, that robs us of the power to control them.

For example, if the weather is rainy and you planned on a picnic, and now you feel upset, is the weather causing your feelings? Or is what you're thinking causing your feelings? Another way to understand this is that on another day you may have the same plan and the weather does the same thing but you don't feel bad. Both times the feelings come from inside.

Which makes more sense to you: that our inner peace is under our control or our inner peace is under other people's control?

If we understand this: In part, I am contributing to my problem, then we have the cure for it.

Long after a bullying or any upsetting event, we can replay and relive the disturbing feelings we felt at the time of the event. We can be haunted for the rest of our lives by one traumatizing event that isn't happening right now. The trauma is stored inside of us but seeing it in a different light releases the emotions and as previously mentioned, leaves the event as a memory available to us to use as a guide to avoid similar events in the future.

As we've discussed, all feelings *pre-exist* inside of us, having been absorbed through the senses in childhood, stored as painful memories, and unknowingly retrieved from the unconscious mind to try to help us during challenges. This process is not easy because we have to face and feel those repressed feelings so they can dissolve. They dissolve once we clearly see them because they are not part of our True Nature. We often don't want to look inside of ourselves because we're scared of what we'll find and worry that we will feel more awful about ourselves. We will do anything to avoid the idea that we're bad. We're not bad if we uncover difficult emotions and bad behaviors—it's our job to uncover them so they don't rule and ruin our experience of life as it unfolds.

For example, if we've had bad experiences with men, is it helpful to dislike all men because of a bad experience with one of them? Is it helpful to have old wounds rubbed into rising up and making us feel awful because we've experienced something painful in the past? Is it helpful to dislike all women for the same reason? It's helpful to dissolve the dislike as the uncomfortable emotion that it is—that exists inside of us and, at the same time—remember the lesson to make us more capable of a better outcome if a similar situation arises.

Our behaviors are learned and can be unlearned. We're unhappy because we have them within us—they are at odds with our Nature—that's why upsets come up—to be dissolved, not to stay lodged in us forever.

Some of the things I've said, like we have a part in bullying if we're the victim are hard to understand. How we know that we have a part is that we are there in the situation.

If someone is physically beaten by another person for no apparent reason, it's not their fault and if they have an energy within them that draws the abuser, they don't know it's there. At the same time, if it is, it makes sense to want to see that and dissolve it asap. If they don't have an attracting energy within them, it won't hurt to look. In my own experience I've always been able to find an unconscious belief that attracts a bullying event that will prove itself to be true: I am a victim.

Doing this work and facing our feelings and our fears is easier than continuing to live as a bully or a victim. In our hearts, we don't want anyone to be a bully or a victim.

Doing The Exercises

Happiness is not ready made.
It comes from your own actions.
-The 14th Dalai Lama

To be effective:

- The exercises must be 'felt', because while an intellectual understanding is important, and these exercises are based in pure intelligence, looking inside of ourselves and seeing (becoming aware of what's in there) is a vital part of dissolving anything that causes us pain. 'Seeing and feeling' what's inside of us *is* what catalyzes change. The truth can't be changed and doesn't need to be so we don't need to worry about dissolving anything that's natural to us (and therefore valuable, like true kindness that doesn't expect or need anything in exchange).

- The feelings that come up are doing so for the purpose of being dissolved. They will no longer be repressed only to express when we least expect or want them.

- The exercises can be repeated until change is observed through your own experiences:

  o The bully disappears out of your life.
  o The bully positively changes their behavior.
  o The bully doesn't change but you aren't hooked into their behavior and don't feel reactive to it.
  o You are clear enough to leave or find help in an abusive situation.

- In all cases, if we're upset, we must acknowledge our part in every dynamic or interaction we're involved in. Some of the exercises ask this of us and as a reward, free us of the energy that attracts a bully.

- All of the strategies are prompting you into awareness because awareness reveals and heals all. It changes how we experience our lives; the more awareness, the more balanced the human being is and a balanced human being doesn't bully or feel victimized. We know this to be true because as soon as we have any information that is based in truth, it changes us. A simple example is that if we're not aware of a shorter route to work, we take the longer one. As soon as we're aware of the shorter route, that information changes us. In this work, we're not aware of ideas that are hidden in our unconscious minds and as soon as we become aware, that changes us. Also, an aware human being cannot hurt themselves or another. To prove this to yourself, remember a time when you felt joyful—can you feel joyful and want to harm someone at the same time?

- In many of the exercises, you are invited to sit quietly with your eyes closed and feel the feelings and sensations and emotions that come up in the mind and body when you think a specific thought. During this contemplation, don't attach to or believe the emotions or thoughts that arise—feel and watch them.

- You may have to repeat the exercises a few or several times to dissolve the layers of beliefs that have been built up over time.

- Do each exercise until you feel a shift into peace. That is the indicator that the exercise has caused all the release that it can for the current session.

Don't Give Up

The sky is not my limit...I am.
-T. F. Hodge

During the exercises, you may:

- Feel strong, uncomfortable emotions; feel them fully until they disappear. If you don't feel anything at first, simply sit and the feelings will arise. We are so used to burying feelings that it may take a few seconds to become aware of them. They have to disappear if they are felt fully because they aren't true and what isn't true can't last if it's seen. All negative feelings are not our True Nature and must disappear if brought into awareness.
- Get strong, uncomfortable thoughts about your past or another person; feel them fully until they dissipate. The mind has a way of linking and building on experiences in our past and when we honestly and simply 'look' at what's in the mind, it brings up associations that can also be unraveled.
- Feel physical sensations, aches, or slight brief pains in the body or brain; observe them—they will disappear, and it's possible the disappearance of the stored emotion can take with them, health issues.
- Want to judge, defend, or justify. The part of the mind that wants to do that is the part that wants you to hang on tight to old beliefs that cause the pain you feel in the first place. Don't judge anything that arises; simply observe and feel.
- Want to stop doing the exercise. That's the inner sufferer speaking. Don't listen.

The Types of Strategies

They did not know it was impossible so they did it.
-Mark Twain

Some strategies help us rid ourselves of experiencing life through the lens of a victim. The victim, although we can't help it (until we're aware of it) and don't know it, is immersed in victimhood because of unconscious beliefs. Unconscious beliefs means we adopted ideas through some childhood experiences (that are stored in memory) that are dictating how we feel now, even though childhood is long gone.

Some strategies are to help others stop bullying us. Many of us have stopped a bully, some of us without ever talking to the bully by doing these types of exercises that help dissolve the energy in us that attracts them.

Some strategies help us stop bullying ourselves. The inner critic comes from the inner perfectionist and the inner punisher, and variations on those themes. They are not pathways to peace.

If you have a child who is a bully, you'll be happy to know that many of these strategies can transition your child from their bullying tendencies back into their playful, loving nature. If they are done in earnest and felt fully, there is no option but to change.

BullyProof Strategy
Don't Believe a Bully

"Never argue with stupid people, they will drag you down
to their level and then beat you with experience."
— Mark Twain

Bullies give terrible advice. They say things like, "You shouldn't have been born." Is a bully in charge of who should be born?

They give you hateful, disapproving and disgusted looks. Don't believe that's about you. Those looks are generated from inside of them. That doesn't need to catalyze your lower nature—don't believe them.

Exercise:

Sit quietly with your eyes closed in a spot you won't be disturbed, and contemplate these questions, inviting yourself to connect to your inner wisdom:

"Does it make sense to believe a bully?"

It makes no sense to believe someone who wants to hurt you.

Exercise:

"But could the bully be right? I feel worthless sometimes."

We are all here and that proves we're all supposed to be here. If we feel worthless, we're believing the wrong thing. If Creation (you insert the name of the one you worship) made us and put us here, it is disrespectful to Creation to think we don't belong.

Exercise:

"Would it be helpful to me to ask another adult or someone I trust for help? What if they think I'm stupid?"

Contemplate this ancient proverb: *A problem shared is a problem halved.*

"Would I feel better if I told someone and got some advice other than the advice the bully is giving me or the advice my own negative thoughts are giving me? I don't have to take to heart or act on any advice that doesn't feel right to me."

Don't believe yourself when you're bullying yourself, either.

BullyProof Strategy
Intervene When You See Bullying Happening

"If you are neutral in situations of injustice, you have chosen the side of the oppressor. If an elephant has its foot on the tail of a mouse, and you say that you are neutral, the mouse will not appreciate your neutrality."
-Desmond Tutu

When it's safe for you to do so, intervene to stop a bully from bullying someone else.

Jackie Chan, a well-known actor and martial artist shares his experience, "I allowed myself to be bullied because I was scared and didn't know how to defend myself. I was bullied until I prevented a new student from being bullied. By standing up for him, I learned to stand up for myself."

Ross Ellis, Founder of Stomp Out Bullying says to authoritatively say, "Stop," and "then take the arm of the victim and lead them away even if the bully is still talking." Bill Belsey, President and Founder of Bullying. org suggests it's good if you have a couple of friends for support when you intervene.

Source: *What to Say To A Bully: 31 Expert Recommendations.* July 31, 2019. Accessed August 20, 2021. https://www.crisisprevention.com/en-CA/Blog/What-Do-You-Say-To-a-Kid-When-They-re-Bullying

If it's safe and you can drum up the courage, you build confidence and help a fellow human being at the same time.

The Youth Project Study says this method can help, do nothing for the situation or make it worse. You must do this in conjunction with the self-inquiry strategies in this book, like I am That, The Turnaround, What's The Gain, Human Sharks, etc. to make the "Stop Strategy" more effective.

BullyProof Strategy
Is There A Time I Shouldn't Intervene?

Good decisions come from experience. Experience
comes from making bad decisions.
-Mark Twain

There may be times you would be wise to not intervene. Some kids don't want their parents interfering and, in some cases, there will be a better outcome if the kids handle the problem for themselves—if it doesn't appear too serious. If you feel that your child is in a situation that can be handled without your help, such as a mild bully on a school bus, a friend who briefly lashes out after they've gone through a stressful experience—respect your child's request so they grow their own authority over bullies.

BullyProof Strategy
Refuse Their Invitation

Do not be bullied out of your common sense...
-Oliver Wendall Holmes

This practice will keep you less reactive when a bully appears.

Exercise:

Think of a bully in your life and silently say, "Your behavior is yours and *I'm not going to react and bring up my own ugliness.*"

BullyProof Strategy
Human Sharks (Bullies)

The smaller the mind,
The greater the conceit.
-Aesop

Vernon Howard, a spiritual teacher, and "an author read and respected by more than 8 million readers" suggests that we are giving a human shark (a bully) something that we must not give.

Exercise:

1. Sit quietly with your eyes closed.
2. Silently name a bully in your life.
3. Ask yourself what s/he wants that you must not give.
4. Wait quietly for an answer to bubble up that feels true for you. *Examples of what might arise: approval, power, attention. When I first did this exercise, I found that I wanted the bully to have power over me, I wanted to submit to them because if I did, then they might not hurt me. If I had power, I felt they would hurt me. It makes a strange kind of sense, as all beliefs initially do, but also show themselves to be damaging instead of helpful.*
5. Feel the emotions and physical sensations that arise but don't let them drag you away. If they are fully felt, they'll dissolve on their own because they are not a part of your Original Nature.
6. Remind yourself that you've been giving what you must not give.
7. Let that come into your awareness the next time you encounter a bully. Notice they are pulling up in bullying behavior and remind yourself that you are no longer going to give them what they want. There is no need to address the bully, just 'know' you're not that same person anymore.
8. Notice if the dynamics between you and the bully change.

Exercise:

Once you've realized what you've given to the bully that you shouldn't have, ask yourself these questions:

1. What is my power?
2. Where is my power?
3. How can I find my power?

1. Why am I seeking approval from abusers. Look at the approval I sought and got and that hasn't solved any problems.
2. Do I need their approval?
3. Why?

1. Why do I need attention from bullies?
2. What kind of attention do I really want?
3. How can I get that.

BullyProof Strategy
Act Like You Mean Business

Worrying is like paying a debt you don't owe.
-Mark Twain

It's almost impossible not to worry about our kids as they go out into the world (even if worrying has never done any good). We will worry less if we find ways to equip our kids with strategies that will help them. I took my daughters to a self-defence class and learned this:

- You are less likely to be attacked (physically or verbally by a perpetrator or a bully) if you walk like you mean business with your head high and your spine straight.
- Catch yourself with your shoulders rolled forward and push them back. Practice the 'Superwoman/man stance'.

If you have kids, you can teach them to walk like Superman or Superwoman on the way to the park. If you have older kids you can invite them to practice walking that way every time they walk from their bedroom to the front door to go to school.

Even if you have to pretend at first, practice these ways of presenting your stronger side towards anyone who may be sizing up the size of the target on your back.

BullyProof Strategy
Tell Them To Stop

Once you strip away that feeling
of invincibility, he can be had.
— *Rocky Marciano*

The bully doesn't expect you to tell them to cut it out or stop it. They've picked you to bully because they don't think you will be able to say those things to them. Surprise them, when you feel like you're not in physical danger by saying and doing the following things:

- "Stop it, now."
- "This is not okay. Stop it."
- "No. Stop it."
- Physically hold your hand out in the universally accepted sign for 'Stop', unless you think your action may put you in physical danger. Sometimes a bully will take words or movement on your part as a challenge and physically attack. Don't do this if you feel that's the case.

The Youth Voice Research Project (mentioned previously) suggests that this strategy can make things better, worse, or there will be no change. **41% of the time, <u>telling the bully to stop</u> made the bullying worse**. It made it better 14% of the time. 46% of the time it made no difference.

THAT'S WHY WE HAVE TO DO INNER WORK IN ADDITION TO THESE CONVENTIONAL STRATEGIES.

Once the bully is gone and you are 100% sure that they can't see or hear you, do the Superman or Superwoman Stance or the Martial Artist cry of 'Hi-ya'.

Some surgeons do the Superman or Superwoman stance before they go into surgery. They put their hands on their hips, stand there with absolute certainty, raise their chin a bit, the body straight and confident—to reinforce I CAN DO THIS. I AM EMPOWERED.

'Hi-ya' is (one of) the martial artist's way of confirming strength. In the context it's used here, it means I AM NOT HELPLESS. I AM NOT POWERLESS.

Once you've bested a bully, you not only *deserve* a Superman or Superwoman Stance or a 'Hi-Ya', but it also reinforces your ability to understand you can take on a challenging situation and come out okay.

Buy a Superman or Superwoman headband. Having the physical headband helps send the message to your brain that you do have inner strength.

In addition, do the strategies: *I am That, The Turnaround and What Do I Gain, Human Sharks, etc.*

BullyProof Strategy
Bullying is What We Know

I've never let my schooling interfere with my education.
-Mark Twain

If we felt bullied when we were little, that becomes the 'norm' and we unconsciously put ourselves in situations where we can experience what we learned was 'normal'—we hang around bullies. We are unconsciously drawn to them because it's what we know. If we were aware of this, we would want it to change.

Sit with these questions and see the ridiculousness and unnaturalness of bullying as being normal:

"Is bullying really 'normal'?"
"Do I have to accept bullying?"
"Is it intelligent to accept abuse from another person?"
"How is it truer that bullying is and *feels abnormal*?"

BullyProof Strategy
Turn Bullying Into Blossoming

"If people throw stones at you,
pick them up and build something."
-Unknown

Nadia Sparkes, a (then) 12-year-old school girl from the U.K. was called Trash Girl by a group of bullies because she picked up trash and empty bottles on her way to school. Besides hurling insults at her, they also threw garbage and other objects at her.

Nadia and her mom started a Facebook page called Team Trash Girl—they took the stones that were thrown at her and built something out of them! At this writing, she had 6.5K members!

Source: https://www.westernjournal.com/teen-called-trash-girl-recycling-response-bullies-poetic/ *The Western Journal, After Teen Called 'Trash Girl' for Recycling, Response To Bullies is Poetic.* Kim Davis. *February 24, 2018.* Accessed August 19, 2021

Exercise:

How can you turn your experience into something that would help someone else?

- Could you donate your time at anti-bullying organizations and share some of these strategies that worked for you?
- Could you start a podcast to help victims change their situation and feelings about their lives?
- Could you start a blog or social media page?
- Could you gather a few people who are around you when you see a bully and ask them to help you approach the bully and intervene?

- Could you write an article about it and ask your local newspaper to include it in their publication?
- Could you write to your government representatives and bring the issue to their attention?

BullyProof Strategy
The Bully Who Lives Inside ALL Of US

Those who dare to fail miserably
can achieve greatly.
-John F. Kennedy

We all have a bully inside of us—it's the inner critic who threatens us, tells us we're not good enough, and even threatens our very lives.

The inner bully also silently attacks others through having nasty thoughts about them. When we attack others, with our thoughts, we don't feel good. Check and see for yourself how you feel when you silently bully another person.

The more we can recognize this inner bully in the moment, the more relief we will experience and the kinder we will be to ourselves and others.

Exercise

This exercise is helpful to banish bully-thoughts we have about ourselves and others. When they arise, use one or more of the strategies offered until you feel relief. As always, feel all the feelings that come up until they dissolve.

Begin to recognize when your inner bully is speaking to you. It says things like this to you about others:

-   "I wish she/he would die (or have an accident or suffer)."
-   "Everybody hates him."

The inner bully says things like this about yourself:

-   "You're no good." (Is a bully an expert on goodness?).

- "I wish I was dead." (The bully in you attacking you. I hope you have a sense of humor: the bully is wishing it's host would die. Your True Nature doesn't feel this way).
- "I should know better." (The bully in you is chastising you).
- "I'm stupid." (Said the bully who thinks it's smart).
- "I'm a waste of skin. My sister said so." (Reminder to not listen to bullies, they're not intelligent).

When these nonsensical, stress-causing bully-thoughts occur, take the inner bully by the horns and say to it:

- "You're not here to help me."
- "You're here to hurt me."
- "You're here to hurt others."
- "You're not the boss of me." (It's a great saying, even if it's for kids—I use it effectively).
- "Stop this, now."
- "Stop, this is not who I am or want to be."
- "I don't agree with you."
- "You have no power over me."
- "This is a passing unhelpful thought, it's not who I am."
- "Thoughts don't need to control me."

Do the strategy called 'What Do I Gain?'

BullyProof Strategy
I Don't Want to Be A Bully

"Being a bully still haunts me."
-Anonymous

Bullies don't want to be bullies. Who gets up in the morning and thinks, "I'm so grateful I get to bully someone today?" Rather, they feel ugly inside of themselves and want to try to get rid of that feeling and they do it by finding someone else they can label as bad and bully them.

Exercise

When you get the urge to:

- Verbally bully yourself or others (insult, judge, be mean etc.).
- Physically bully yourself or others (push, hit, self-harm, etc.).
- Socially bully others (shame someone publicly, join in a mob, etc.).
- Cyberbully (bully others using the internet).

1. Say and feel the truth of the statement until the feelings and images that arise pass:
   o "I am acting like a bully."
   o "I want to hurt other people."
   o "Other people have hurt me, so I think it's okay to hurt them. Is it true that it's okay to hurt others?"
   o "My form of justice is to lash out at the other person, so my form of justice is injustice because lashing out doesn't cause justice to happen. It causes more injustice."
2. Ask yourself, "Does this feel natural, like a part of my nature?"
3. Remind yourself, "I am suffering right now because of what I want to do."
4. Remind yourself, "I am going to suffer when I hurt another person because of karmic laws which state that actions have

consequences attached to them." The action of harming another has the action of harming ourselves attached to it. You can become aware of that by noticing how you feel inside when you bully someone. You don't *feel* natural which proves bullying isn't natural.

5. Remove yourself and as self-care expert, Suzi Lula (<u>www. suzilula.com</u>) says, take a few minutes to get some distance by saying, 'I need a moment'.
    o   Go to another room and do deep breathing.
    o   Go outside and take a walk or run.
    o   Do as many of the strategies in the book as you can to help yourself come back into your peaceful nature.
6. Do the Superman or Superwoman stance or 'Hi-Ya' to reinforce that you can dissolve your own inner bully. You are not powerless against your inner bully.
7. Do the HeartMath Quick Coherence® Technique (reprinted with permission from www.heartmath.com):

"Step 1: Focus your attention in the area of the heart. Imagine your breath is flowing in and out of your heart or chest area, breathing a little slower and deeper than usual.

Suggestion: Inhale 5 seconds, exhale 5 seconds (or whatever rhythm is comfortable).

Step 2: Make a sincere attempt to experience a regenerative feeling such as appreciation or care for someone or something in your life.

Suggestion: Try to re-experience the feeling you have for someone you love, a pet, a special place, an accomplishment, etc. or focus on a feeling of calm or ease."

To dissolve an upset, do this for several minutes. Repeat it until you feel calm.

Do HeartMath or any other calming technique several times a day to bring you back to your nature. You might even be able to do it next time someone confronts you so you can stay in a sane state when others aren't.

BullyProof Strategy
Consequences of Bullying

*"What if the kid you bullied at school, grew up, and turned
out to be the only surgeon who could save your life?"*
-Lynette Mather

If you child is, or you are, a bully, spend some time considering the consequences (because they're there).

Here are some to ponder:

1. What if karma is true (and it is)? The word karma means action. All actions have consequences automatically attached to them. Some examples are: If you go outside without an umbrella and it's raining, you get wet. If you don't hand in an assignment on time, you have some free time, possibly get in trouble or lose credibility. If you bully someone badly enough, you will lose them, they will charge you under the law, or they'll use physical violence against you that damages you.

Questions:

-   "Am I okay with the trouble I'm going to bring upon myself?"
-   "Will I let whatever karma I've unleashed by bullying someone turn me into a victim?"

2. Bullying can have legal consequences.

Questions:

-   "If someone else severely bullied my family members, would I want them to be charged under the law?"
-   "Am I willing to accept that I may be charged under the law and that is just a consequence I'm willing to bear?"

3. Bullying ruins relationships.

Questions:

- "Do I want to damage or possibly destroy relationships?"
- "Am I okay with the possible misery that will bring me? My mind will bring up over and over how bad the one I bullied is and I'll feel stress. Is that okay with me?"
- "Am I okay if I lose family, friends or a job because of bullying?"

4. Bullying is often violent.

Questions:

- "Do I want to be violent?"
- "What do I think I gain if I'm violent?"
- "If I have kids, do I want them to be violent?"
- "Am I okay if someone commits suicide because I bullied them?"

BullyProof Strategy
The Turnaround (Byron Katie)

A lie can travel half way around the world
while the truth is putting on its shoes.
-Mark Twain

An effective way to get the target off of our backs if we're being bullied is to use Katie's work. You can access her work at www.thework.com. In this exercise we use one part of her work to bring us relief.

Katie explains that whatever is happening, is happening for us, to help us see something about ourselves that we wouldn't otherwise see. That means we need to use the experience to dig out something inside of us that causes us pain. That means that whatever happens is for us to *see what's left in us* that's causing pain. If there is any negative behavior left in us, we will see it in someone else and take that as an opportunity to dissolve it in us.

It's true that any moment that upsets us has a hidden gift—the gift is that if we use one of these mind awakening strategies, we will dissolve stress because it dissolves the belief that's causing the stress, feel free, and then our experience of life will be one of feeling safe and whole.

Exercise

Make a very long list accusing the bully in the harshest manner you can. Don't hold back. This will dissolve those same character flaws in you that you don't want anymore, anyway.

Examples:

The bully is mean.
The bully is terrifying.
The bully is aggressive.
The bully is dangerous.
The bully is self-centered.

The bully gets away with things s/he shouldn't.
The bully hurts me.

Turn each statement around towards yourself.
I am mean.
I am terrifying.
I am aggressive.
I am dangerous.
I am self-centered.
I get away with things I shouldn't.
I hurt me.

Once you've turned the statement around to you, find out where you have acted like that. Wait, with your eyes closed, for the answer to arise. It may come in images or thoughts, but if you wait, you will be able to see where you've acted exactly like that. It will come with feelings that are uncomfortable. Feel them until they disappear, taking with them, the belief that causes the urge to act out.

Example:

I am mean. (I was mean to my neighbor when I didn't speak to her.)
I am terrifying. (I was terrifying to my kids when I spanked them.)
I am aggressive. (I was aggressive towards my partner when I hollered at him.)
I am dangerous. (I was dangerous when I drove too fast.)
I am self-centered. (I am self-centered when I make everything about me—try not talking about yourself for long periods of time when speaking with another person to demonstrate this.)
I get away with things I shouldn't. (I got away with spanking my kids.)
I hurt me. (When I spanked my kids, it hurt me to do that.)

Exercise:

Now we turn the statement around again.
The next turnaround is "I am mean to the bully."

Do the same for the following statements, feeling all the feelings that arise until they dissolve. Describe how the following is true:

I am mean to the bully.
I am terrifying to the bully.
I am aggressive to the bully.
I am dangerous to the bully.
I am self-centered and don't consider the bully.
I get away with things I shouldn't against the bully.
I hurt the bully.

BullyProof Strategy
I Am That

You cannot swim for new horizons until you
have courage to lose sight of the shore.
-William Faulkner

This exercise helps to dissolve the bully in us and shoo away the characteristics inside of us that attracts a bully—and turn us into a bully!

Don't throw the book away when you read this: the exercise is based on the ancient wisdom that the outer world reflects the inner world. That means the upset (bully experience) happened, in part, for you to see that you are a bully and that the behavior in the other person is coming to your attention for the purpose of dissolving it in you—because it's in you. This is good news—it's how we can run the bullying tendencies out of us.

You can deny but can't disprove this because someone else will be happy to tell you where you've bullied others if you're not willing to see it for yourself—just ask them.

If we're honest, we know that we have bullied ourselves and others and we also know that we don't want to do that anymore.

These are some things we know about a bully:

- They lash out at others.
- They hate.
- They act angry and don't know how to deal with it.
- They are insecure.
- They are afraid.
- They are mean.
- They are pushy.
- They are arrogant.

The little book of peaceful power.

- They are unfeeling.
- They don't have empathy or compassion.
- They want power and authority.
- They are powerful.
- They have all the power.

Exercise

Sit quietly, with your eyes closed.

1. Say each statement below separately and quietly to yourself.
2. Let images or words come up in your mind that show you where you have behaved or felt that way.
3. Feel the feelings that arise and feel them until they dissipate (if you raise and feel the stored feeling, it has the opportunity to release).
4. 'They lash out at others' becomes 'I lash out at others.'

    - I lash out at others.
    - I hate.
    - I act angry and don't know how to deal with it.
    - I am insecure.
    - I am afraid.
    - I am mean.
    - I am pushy.
    - I am arrogant.
    - I am unfeeling.
    - I don't have empathy or compassion.
    - I want power and authority.
    - I am powerful.
    - I have all the power.

5. Next time you encounter a bully, write down everything you can think of and accuse them harshly and then do this exercise to free yourself of similar behaviors. You will feel relief even when you think about the bully. If you don't, repeat the exercise with whatever comes up when you think about the bully.

BullyProof Strategy
Self-Regulating After a Bully Bullies You

Do what you can't
-Casey Neistat

Every time, after you get to safety, don't do nothing—do self-care:

- If you're shaking, after a bullying experience, don't try to stop it. It's there to dissolve the adrenaline rush. Let it stop naturally.
- Do the HeartMath Quick Coherence® Technique (described earlier) or another breathing technique to bring you back into a calm and coherent state.
- Record & report as mentioned earlier. Don't stay silent.
- Do the following BullyProof Strategies:
  o I am That
  o What do I Gain If I'm Bullied?
  o The Turnaround
  o Dissolve Yourself to The Other's Problems
  o Any other exercises you are drawn to.
  o Blessing Mistakes—even though the bully doesn't know any better, and, they are still responsible for his/her behavior—bullying is a mistake. Aside from that, you want to set yourself free of the upsetting feeling of blame, and this helps. "That bully matters more than their mistake of bullying. They are human beings who hurt badly and that's why they hurt others. I hope they can get help for their pain. I forgive them for my own sake."
  o If you acted out in reaction, say and feel the truth of the statement, "I matter more than this mistake of reacting to a bully." It's difficult to have no reaction to a bully, but the negative feelings don't need to last for long.
  o Put your Superwoman/man headband on and say, "I am not powerless against them."

The little book of peaceful power.

- If you feel like you were powerless against them, use Blessing Mistakes on yourself, "I matter more than the mistake of thinking, speaking and acting like I'm powerless. I'm a work in progress and that's okay."

BullyProof Strategy
Victims Are Violent (Yes, we are)

*Courage is not the absence of fear, but rather the assessment
that something else is more important than fear.*
-Franklin D. Roosevelt

We are unknowingly in a boxing ring with a bully, and it makes us violent. That's not a consequence of being bullied that we expected.

If we believe we're a victim and don't do anything to bring ourselves into awareness, we become violent. As Byron Katie says, "Victims are the most violent people on the planet."

We can bring understanding to that statement by contemplating it: when we believe we've been harmed, we lash out. Think about war torn countries. One person harms another and now they are a victim. The harmed one (the victim) lashes out and harms someone else (who becomes a victim) who then lashes out to harm someone else, until that disastrous philosophy spreads across a whole nation.

In your own life, think about the one who harmed you. What would you like to do to them? We don't want to welcome them into our home, extend them compassion, or sing their praises. We want them to hurt. Be honest here so you can set yourself free.

Who you are is not a victim. Your nature is joyfully harmless. Remember, how you know that to be true is that when you're in those states, you *feel* natural.

There is no good reason to stay in victim mentality: it's painful in every way. That's why I say to use every bullying incident for your benefit—meet and defeat the bully, don't let them make you a violent victim.

Exercise

Dissolve the Violent Victim

Even if you have been bullied, you don't want to be violent because it won't help.

1. Think of a bully in your life.
2. Recall their crime against you (how they bullied you).
3. Get quiet and ask yourself to show you how you lashed out at them and became violent (in thoughts or actions).
4. Ask yourself to see where you've been violent to someone other than the victim after you were bullied.
5. Feel all the feelings that arise without attaching to them.

Exercise

Feel **the truth of these statements:**

"I no longer wish to be a victim."
"I no longer wish to be violent."
"I'm so sorry I've been identified with a violent victim mentality, I didn't know."

BullyProof Strategy
What Do I Gain If I'm Bullied?

> *You have power over your mind—not outside events.*
> *Realize this, and you will find strength.*
> *-Marcus Aurelius*

If we can be honest (and we want to because we really want to end bullying) we have to see that we are unconsciously participating in an unknown need to be treated in that way.

To explain further, if I'm attached to victimhood, I'm unconsciously attached to bullies and abusers so I can uphold my victimhood. I can't be a victim without them being a bully, so I need them (without consciously wanting that situation). I'd vehemently deny that I wanted them in my life, and yet, this work will prove otherwise. You have to stick with it, though, and not be drawn into rejecting this idea or you're back where you started, leaving the reasons for the bullying hidden in your unconscious mind.

Ridiculous, But True Examples:

- We need bullies (who look bad) in our lives so we can feel as though we look good (like a saint or an angel). If a bully acts out against us or another, by comparison, we look pretty good and can hide our own insecurities. We would only need to 'look good' if we were insecure ourselves.
- If we believe that we need to be strong, we will unconsciously invite bullying so we can prove we are strong and can 'take' anything. It's one (unnecessary way) to prove strength.
- We learn that victims get help from others in life, and in that case, we will unconsciously attract bullies so we can be a victim and get help. When we were little and got badly hurt by someone, we got help. That grew, unchecked, into unconsciously believing that was a way to get help.

- Another common gain that we have (unknowingly) is if we are bullied, we are innocent. Our nature is that already, we don't need bullies in our lives to prove that.

While it brings up upsetting feelings in the moment, we look at what we gain when we're bullied, this is one of the easiest and fastest ways to dissolve the beliefs hidden in our unconscious mind that unknowingly attract bullies.

These unconscious ways of thinking no longer serve. They may have *seemed* to be helpful when we were children, but they don't help now.

We can get help, be good, innocent and strong
without being a victim.

Exercise

Think of a bully in your life.

Sit with and feel the truth of the statement:

"I look good when _____ (fill in the name of the bully) looks bad." That means I actually (without knowing this) want him/her to look bad. I tell people how bad he/she is and that's how I know I want them to look bad. It's ridiculous for me to think my 'goodness' arises out of another's 'badness'. Our nature is naturally good.

Notice it's not really a truth, is it? We don't really want the other to look bad; that can't help any situation. That sentiment doesn't feel natural to us. How we know that to be true is to get quiet and feel how we feel inside when we say, "I want the bully to look bad." We don't feel natural, and that's how we know it's not natural to think and feel that way.

This is an example of how bullies come into our lives:

We're a little kid.

We get bullied by a sibling, parent, relative, etc.

The bully looks bad.

The mind (without it being obvious) figures out that if the other person is bullying and bad, since we're not the one bullying then we're good.

Therefore, we look good (in comparison to the bully).

According to this logic, one way to stop bullies is to:

-   See that needing to look good, angelic, pure or better than them comes from insecurity. *Feel what insecurity feels like right now.*
-   Notice needing someone to take pity on you. *Feel what pity feels like right now.*
-   See that you are unconsciously believing the way to get help or love from others is to be hurt. *Feel what it feels like to have this belief inside of you: "I need to get hurt so I can get help."* You could skip the 'needing to get hurt 'and go straight to getting help when you need it.
-   See that you are thinking you're strong if you're bullied. You're innately psychologically strong. *Feel what that feels like: you may as well wear a tee shirt that says: 'Bully me so I can stand up for myself and show everyone how strong I am'.*

BullyProof Strategy
Inclusiveness Ends Bullying

Imagine the words you speak end up on your skin.
Would you be more careful with what you say?
-Unknown

In his article, *Bullying—In Conflict With Existence,* Sadhguru explains that **everything in existence, right down to an atom is not here exclusively and requires other life for it to exist.** Source: Sadhguru, The Isha Foundation, *Bullying—In Conflict With Existence.* Accessed: November 19, 2021.

How does this relate to bullying? When we begin to see the inclusiveness that life actually is, our wrong and painful thinking switches from judging and excluding others to joyful acceptance and inclusiveness— from a happy place there is no impulse to bully or hurt another life. When you feel truly alive, you are in right relationship with life and suffering disappears. When you feel like bullying or in any other negative state, you are in a state of conflict with life and pain comes.

Life is inclusive in these ways:

- You are a parent because of a child. It's an inclusive relationship. One includes the other.
- Soil, seeds, farmers, rain, the earth, the sun and the space that holds it all are inclusive in order to make food for our tables. Another way to say this is food production requires each of these contributing factors.
- The birds, the sky, and the tree involve each other. They don't exist independently, they exist inclusively.
- The sun includes the earth, the moon, and all other planets in the orbiting process.

Life itself is inclusive. Could you live here alone? One way to become a little humbler is to think about it this way: this life is including you. The earth and life-giving air are including you. Gratitude and harmlessness can arise if that is understood deeply.

If you understand inclusiveness, you can't bully anyone. As Sadhguru teaches, you naturally respect all of life.

Exercise:

Here are two ways human beings are naturally included in life and are inclusive:

1. They're here. They are alive so they are already included by something more powerful than your ideas. (Excluding them is going against life).
2. Kids include everyone; they don't register and aren't informed by skin color, body size, or status. They don't care about any of those things if you sit down in a sandbox to play with them. They are naturally inclusive *because it's natural.*

Can you think of more ways that inclusiveness is the way the world works?

Be Inclusive—it's natural.

BullyProof Strategy
"Not-Wanted-Right-Now"

The most courageous act is to think for yourself. Aloud.
-Coco Chanel

Dr. Wayne Dyer, American self-help speaker and author, in his article, *Just Say No to Turmoil* succinctly sums up the ego's intentions:

"Your ego will push you in the direction of the fight. You must be ready to see it as it is about to happen and invite your higher self to send your ego a 'not-wanted-right-now' message. Know within that you always have the choice. When you opt for turmoil and anxiety, you allow your ego to take over. You can instead be a home for peace."

Source: Dr. Wayne Dyer, *Just Say No to Turmoil*. Accessed: November 19, 2019. https://www.drwaynedyer.com/blog/just-say-no-to-turmoil/

Exercise

The moment you feel like you are going to be drawn into a fight with a bully (or anyone else), imagine a window pops up on the screen of your mind and says: "Ego, you're not wanted right now."

BullyProof Strategy
Volunteer The Bully Behavior Out

The two most important days of your life are the day
you are born and the day you find out why.
-Mark Twain

Whether you or your child is being bullied, or is a bully, find someplace to volunteer to help others. This is based on the simple and ancient Hindu philosophy: *When you help your brother's boat to the shore, you arrive there too.* Find kid-friendly organizations near you.

Ideas for Places to Volunteer

- Organize a local, regular clean up of a park or common area.
- See if the local assisted living facility needs volunteers.
- Hospitals often need volunteers.
- Volunteer at any charitable organization.
- Walk dogs for the animal shelter.
- Find or start a community garden.
- Read to, write letters for, run errands for, or clean for seniors.
- Write letters to people in your community, city, and country thanking them for what they do.

Giving is natural and brings out our inborn humanitarianism.

BullyProof Strategy
I'm Not Good Enough

Whether you think you can or you can't, you're right.
-Henry Ford

When we're little, we learn ideas like "I'm not good enough"

- When we get into trouble.
- When someone frowns at us.
- When we perceive others are better than us.
- When we don't do well on tests, sports, conversations, or other situations that we feel are challenging.
- When we make mistakes.
- When we believe another's negativity is about us.

Where's the proof that we're not good enough?

Doesn't every single human being on the planet struggle with the same issues we do—at different times in their lives? Are they good enough?

Exercise

Sit quietly with your eyes closed and say and feel the truth of the statement: "I am enough." Feel any feelings that arise until they fall away. Repeat it until you have a deep inner feeling that you are enough.

You are.

BullyProof Strategy
If Your Child is A Bully

Courage is grace under pressure.
-Ernest Hemingway

It's so understandable (Suzi Lula's beautifully connecting and compassionate statement) that it hurts when you notice your child is a bully, or when someone else informs you of that unfortunate state of affairs. We didn't become parents to raise bullies. Take heart, it's curable!

Besides doing all the exercises in this book yourself, these are things you can do for and with your child. Do the strategies you prefer and add in the others until you see change in your child.

- Learn more about what's going on in their lives. Are they trying to fit in, do they need more attention, are their friends a good, stable influences or not?
- Since it's true that those who hurt others do so because they hurt inside of themselves, talk with them about what hurts them.

The bully has a need that isn't being met and it's often attention. Give your child your undivided attention frequently.

- Teach them to notice that they don't like to be hurt or bullied and that's a good reason to not bully anyone else.
- Teach them that who they are is not their behavior in the same way they are not their feelings—these states come and go, but what is seeing them is always here.
- Ask them to notice that their bullying doesn't bring them joy or peace and those are states they truly love.
- Ensure they feel accepted and loved; encourage them by pointing out how valuable they are to the family and make special note of their talents.

- Find ways to relieve the stress they feel. Learn the strategies in *The Kid Code, 30 Second Parenting Strategies* and then teach your kids how to de-stress the moment an upset arises—instead of acting out.
- Help them develop their social skills, by practicing them.
- Ask your kids to share these ideas with other kids so they have allies, and at the same time, offer to others a different way to be in the world.
- After they've calmed down after bullying someone, ask your child what bothers them ask them why they feel they need to behave in that way. The simple question, "Why?" can sometimes reach a bully.

As you will see later in the book, WestEd, a non-profit organization dedicated to enhancing human experience, demonstrates proof that restorative justice decreases bullying. Ubuntu, explained below, (and Blessing Mistakes) are the practical application of restorative justice which is a process that maintains the dignity of everyone involved in a conflict.

- Perform Ubuntu. The kind and inclusive South African philosophy and intervention is designed to bring the one who has done wrong back into their natural and good nature by putting them in a circle of their peers and everyone telling them of all the good they have done. This brings out the good in them and makes them want to behave in ways that serve everyone and at the same time, it makes them want to make up for what they've done. We can adapt this philosophy—we don't have to put them in a circle, but by doing this for just a few minutes a few times a week, it will help them feel secure.
- As their parent, bless your child's mistake of being a bully by saying to them, "You matter more than the mistake of bullying."
- Teach your child to say and feel the truth of the statement, "I matter more than the mistake of bullying." And teach them to

make it right—get them to truly feel the apology they make to those they've bullied.

- Do Susan Stiffleman's (a well-known marriage and family therapist) 'Love Flooding Method' invites you to write down 10 things you genuinely love about the child and share that with them privately.
- Say to your child, "I don't respond to that behavior, and in truth, neither do you. That's not who you are and you can tell that be seeing how you feel inside of yourself."
- Do your own inner work on whatever comes up in you about the child's behavior, or about other's who are involved. Some of the most effective strategies for releasing stress and behaviors that don't serve us are: I am That, The Turnaround, What's The Gain, and Dissolve Yourself to The Other's Problems.
- Get professional help that ensures their dignity is maintained—if you feel they need it.

Ways to provide security for your child if they are a bully.

Find things they love to do and make sure they do them as much as possible. Put time on your calendar to make sure it gets done. This gives them a sense of accomplishment, worth and security.

Things my child loves to do and is good at:

_____

_____

_____

_____

There is a more in-depth Support Sheet on the website www. thekidcode.ca

BullyProof Strategy
If Your Child is Being Bullied

Never think that war, no matter how necessary,
nor how justified is not a crime.
-Ernest Hemingway

We can feel as devastated and helpless as our child when they are being bullied. These strategies will help.

Ways to provide security for your child if they are being bullied:

Besides doing all the exercises in this book yourself, these are things you can do for and with your child:

- Learn more about what's going on in their lives. Are they trying to fit in, do they need more attention, are their friends a good, stable influence or not?
- Teach them that bullies are not bad people, they are people with bad behaviors—and that doesn't excuse bullies, it makes them more understandable.
- Teach your child that there are many strategies to use to get the target off of their backs.
- Ensure they feel accepted and loved in their family; encourage them by pointing out how valuable they are to the family and make special note of their talents.
- Find ways to relieve the stress they feel. Learn the strategies in *The Kid Code, 30 Second Parenting Strategies* and then teach your kids how to de-stress the moment an upset arises.
- Help them develop their social skills, by practicing them.
- Ask your kids to share these ideas with other kids so they have informed allies.
- After they've calmed down after being bullied by someone and you've used some of the strategies in this book to bring sanity

and serenity back, ask your child what might help them more next time?

- An insecure child has a need that isn't being met and it's often attention. Give your child your undivided attention frequently.
- Perform an adapted form of Ubuntu. The security-building South African philosophy and intervention is designed to draw out the victim's confident nature by putting them in a circle of their peers and everyone telling them of all the good they have done. We can adapt this philosophy—we don't have to put them in a circle, but by doing this for just a few minutes a few times a week, it will help them feel secure.
- Do Susan Stiffleman's 'Love Flooding Method'. Write down 10 things you genuinely love about the child and share that with them in private.
- As their parent, bless their mistake of being identified with victimhood.
- Invite the child to say and feel the truth of the statement, "I matter more than the mistake of believing in victimhood." They can make that right by working every upset and that will deliver them back to their joyfully harmless and playful nature.
- Depending on their age, explain the difference between their True Nature (a natural state where there is no upset feeling) and an identified state (believing a thought that causes stress, such as "I am a victim."). None of us can do better until we know how and have experienced success with strategies like the ones found in this book and others that are similar.
- Do your own inner work on whatever comes up in you about the child's behavior, or about other's who are involved. Some of the most effective strategies for releasing stress and behaviors that don't serve us are: I am That, The Turnaround, What's The Gain, and Dissolving Ourselves to The Other's Problems.
- Get professional help that ensures their dignity is maintained if you feel they need it.

The little book of peaceful power.

- Record and report to the appropriate authorities. This will show the child being bullied that you are supporting them and that there are others who will also support them.
- Find things they love to do and make sure they do them as much as possible. Put it on your calendar to make sure it gets done. This gives them a sense of accomplishment, worth and security.

Things my child loves to do and is good at:

_____

_____

_____

_____

There is a more in-depth Support Sheet on the website www. thekidcode.ca

BullyProof Strategy
Violent Video Games

Where did they learn it's okay to attack any time they want?
-Anonymous

Bullyingcanada.ca says that "research shows that 93% of video games reward violent behavior."

Source: *Get Help*. Accessed August 18, 2021. https://www.bullyingcanada. ca/get-help/

Everyone knows that violence teaches violence. You're the parent, tell them no. You have that authority. When they rebel, offer to help them find games they love that aren't violent.

Kids' emulate what they see; everybody who had kids knows this: monkey see, monkey do. Let them see non-violence instead of violence.

As we've learned, from a consciousness perspective, all the information that our senses take in from the time of birth to the present moment is stored in the unconscious mind and will surface in some way: nightmares, bad behaviors, bad language, and/or mental and emotional disorders.

For example, if you saw a frightening act in a movie, it's stored in the unconscious mind and is going to come out when you least expect it— but you won't link it to the movie. It will just scare you and you'll feel bad for having the thought that was imprinted there earlier. If you saw a person drowning, years later, you may get a thought about someone you love drowning and have the unwanted and untrue thought that it's going to happen and, even worse, it's okay in an unfathomable and guilt-causing way. This is not your thought. It's *absorbed thoughts* that are regurgitating. You're not bad when you have these thoughts. When one appears, keep repeating, "I'm sorry I'm identified with that ridiculous and untrue thought," until you feel a release.

BullyProof Strategy
Role Playing with Your Kids

Your life only gets better when you get better.
-Brian Tracy

If your child is familiar with the tactics a bully relies on, they won't automatically believe a bully when one appears. Role playing will help keep bullies on their radar so they know what to do when one shows up.

Take turns role playing with your child. Use your own judgment and decide on the age-appropriate language and strategies to use.

Teach them these things bullies regularly say (hate speech) so they can identify a bully:

- You're stupid.
- You're a freak.
- You're an idiot.
- You're ugly.
- You're a (cry) baby.
- You're a moron.
- You're useless.
- Nobody likes you.
- You shouldn't have been born.
- You don't belong here.
- Go back to the hole you crawled out of.
- Go back to the country you came from.
- You were a mistake.
- Nobody would care if you died.
- I hate you.
- Everybody hates you, even your own mom.
- Go kill yourself.
- Just kidding.

- Can't you take a joke?
- No offence.

Bullies will repeatedly:

- Say and do mean or cruel things.
- Physically threaten others.
- Threaten to or spread malicious gossip that's not true.
- Make their victims out to be bad—twist the truth.
- Gaslight their victims (the bully is crazy but says the victim is the one that's crazy or off).
- Tease and make fun of others.
- Try to make people do something they don't want to.
- Act aggressively.

BullyProof Strategy
Dissolving Ourselves To The Other's Problems

I can't change the direction of the wind, but I can
adjust my sails to always reach my destination.
-Jimmy Dean

This simple and amazingly effective technique based on the work of Guy Finley, American self-help author, teaches us to dissolve ourselves to the other person's problems. This work removes much of the stress the victim feels.

1. Close your eyes and think of a bully and *their problem* of being a bully.
2. Dissolve yourself to their problem of being a bully. Imagine cutting ties to their problem of bullying. Imagine the ties to the problem melting away.
3. Wish them the best from your heart—they must be in terrible pain to be acting like a bully (wouldn't you love everyone to wish the best for you when you have a problem?). If we were on our death bed, we'd be likely to let go of all anger and be more willing to wish them the best. Let go now and wish them the best.
4. Think of the bully again and if there is any animosity left in your, do the exercise again.
5. Use this every time you encounter a bully.
6. Also, use this strategy when you see a behavior in another person that you don't like (for example, if your child is aggressive, argumentative, etc.).

BullyProof Strategy
The Buddhist Philosophy About Bullies

Be kind for everyone you meet is fighting a hard battle.
-Plato

Buddhism suggests that *we see the suffering a bully experiences* and treat them kindly while seeing to our own self-preservation. If we can truly see suffering in another person, it naturally brings up compassion without obliterating the awareness to keep ourselves safe.

Exercise

1. Think of a bully in your life.
2. Sit quietly with your eyes closed and ask to see why they suffer.
3. Feel all the feelings that arise (to dissolve them).

When I did this exercise, I saw that the bully thought he was dumb and without purpose. That brought up compassion in me and that feels better than hatred towards the bully.

BullyProof Strategy
Buddhist Mantra's

You will never reach higher ground
if you are always pushing others down.
-Unknown

Buddhists also suggest mantras. One of the most popular mantras, *Om mani padme hum*, is said to calm fears, among other documented psychological and physiological health benefits. Look up and listen to several of them until you find one that resonates strongly with you.

BullyProof Strategy
Buddhist 'Cut-Off'

*Always be a first-rate version of yourself, instead of
a second-rate version of somebody else.*
-July Garland

Another Buddhism strategy is called cut-off, meaning cut off any of our own negativity in response to a bully. This helps you stay in your joyfully harmless nature and not be drawn into the realm of the bully's negativity.

Exercise:

Use the strategy taught by Dr. David Hawkins, M.D., Ph.D. for letting go in his book of the same name to cut off negative emotions:

1. The moment you feel a negative thought or emotion arise, become aware it's there and without judgment, let it do what it does until it's processed itself out of you.
2. You may get bigger emotions, thoughts and images of your past or made-up future—do the same with them.

BullyProof Strategy
Prayer or Chanting

It is our choices…that show what we truly are,
far more than our abilities.
-*J. K. Rowling*

Using whichever religion your ascribe to, pray for the bully and yourself.

Find soothing chants or prayers that are in alignment with your religious or spiritual beliefs.

BullyProof Strategy
Asking The Universe for Help

*For me, I am driven by two main philosophies: know more today about
the world that I knew yesterday and lessen the suffering for others.*
-Neil deGrasse Tyson

Many modern spiritual teachers suggest that if we tap into the intelligence
that operates the Universe, we can change our experience of life.

Exercise:

1. Sit quietly with your eyes closed for a few minutes every day.
2. Ask Universal Intelligence to help you solve this problem.
3. Feel gratitude for it, as though it's already done.
4. See yourself as bully-free or no longer a victim and feel gratitude
   for that.

BullyProof Strategy
Truths

When a toxic person can longer control you, they will try to control how others see you. The misinformation will feel unfair, but stay above it, trusting that other people will eventually see the truth just like you did.
-Unknown

Remind yourself of these truths every day a few times a day when you are enmeshed in a bullying experience.

- "My True Nature knows what to do if someone bullies me."
- "I am not what the bully needs for their 'fix'. I'm not identified with weakness, powerlessness or victimhood."
- "I am not better than or less than anyone."

BullyProof Strategy
Reporting A Bully is Self-Preservation

Those who can make you believe absurdities
can make you commit atrocities.
-Voltaire

If you are being bullied, it's an injustice.

Make sure you tell an authority or a professional. The bully needs help and so do you. You don't know if it will help the bully or not, but you need to help yourself. Doing nothing can ensure they keep bullying and that's not in your best interests. Tell a person who can help you. Along with the other strategies, it can definitely help.

The bully will call you a tattletale. Is self-preservation a weakness?

Remember the first strategy: don't believe a bully, they say stupid things. A bully wants you to think telling on them makes you wrong. The bully is wrong.

Exercise:

Remind yourself of this truth: the bully is demonstrating damaging and dangerous behaviors (towards him/herself and others). No one is allowed to put me in danger. It's intelligent to tell the authorities or someone who can help me.

BullyProof Strategy
What Do I Gain?

A ship is safe in harbor, but that's not what ships are for.
-William G. T. Shedd

Pull back the curtain on The Wizard of Oz.

The bully needs the victim to be scared of them (cowardly). Remember Dorothy in The Wizard of Oz. There was so much fear until Toto, Dorothy's dog pulls back the curtain hiding the Wizard, revealing empty, powerless threats. Don't believe the bully is powerful, believe the truth: they are insecure and weak.

This strategy reveals what is in the unconscious mind that draws a perfect target on your back—a GPS for a bully.

Exercise:

Sit quietly with your eyes closed and ask yourself this question, waiting for a *positive word* to arise (dismiss the negative words that arise):

"What do I gain if I am cowardly, bullied?"

You may get answers like:

- I won't step on anyone's toes and therefore, I'll be safe. Notice that not stepping on anyone's toes didn't keep you safe. The formula stored in the unconscious mind doesn't keep you safe.
- They won't hurt me if I'm cowardly. Notice that they did hurt you even when you acted cowardly and were a victim.
- I'm not hurting anyone if I'm cowardly (except myself).

BullyProof Strategy
Malicious Gossiping Is A Form of Bullying

What if the kid you bullied at school, grew up, and turned
out to be the only surgeon who could save your life?
-Unknown

Harsh and harmful gossiping about another is one way the bully inside of us strikes out.

Exercise:

1. Recall the last time you maliciously gossiped, maligned another human being, or wanted to.
2. Notice and feel the *feeling* of malicious 'gossiping' until it passes, taking with it the belief that finding something wrong with another person makes you better than them.

Imagine doing something productive that you love to do instead of gossiping. Imagine talking about something *constructive* instead of gossiping.

We innately know that gossiping is not right. There are many other things we can talk about with our friends and others:

- Positive things that interest us.
- Positive things that interest them.
- Positive or conscious documentaries.
- Solution oriented ideas for mutual problems.
- Strategies we've learned that are self-empowering.
- Good places to get out into nature.
- Interesting local discoveries.
- Local places to volunteer.
- Positive world events.
- Celebrities or influencers who are doing good in the world.
- Great self-help books.
- Anything that's uplifting and positive.

The little book of peaceful power.

BullyProof Strategy
Bless Their Mistake

"Knowing what's right doesn't mean much
unless you do what's right."
-Theodore Roosevelt

Bullying is not in our nature, therefore, it's a mistake. That means when a bully bullies, they are making a mistake.

One day I was driving my dad's too-big truck in his too-small corral and put a dent in it. When I apologized and showed him, he opened his arms wide for me to walk into for a hug. On that day I began to learn to give myself and others Grace, not grief when a mistake is made. Silently, when the bully is not around, say to them, "You, the human being matters more than this mistake of bullying me." All human beings matter more than their mistake.

This is for you to release your angst towards the bully. There can be great resistance to blessing a bully, so if that's the case, say and feel the truth of the statement, "I matter more than being unable to bless or forgive another human being." Then ask yourself if you could say and feel the truth of the statement, "They matter more than their mistake."

If you still can't do it, notice you are the one who refuses to forgive and are therefore choosing to carry hatred around inside of you. We don't need that anymore. Feel what it feels like inside of you to be unable to forgive or feel hatred—feel it as deeply as you can so it dissolves. Say and feel the truth of the statement, "I matter more than the mistake of harboring dislike or hatred towards another human being."

We want to release our own internal discomfort because it's not good for us to carry that.

Who knows, maybe with some blessings they'll stop bullying. Maybe not. But if you do this exercise, you'll feel better and that's one of our goals—wellbeing for ourselves.

The little book of peaceful power.

BullyProof Strategy
Ubuntu – Build Security in The Bully and The Victim

Love is fatal to identification.

This strategy can cure the bully and the victim mentality or at least knock some of it out. This strategy is useful for the parents of a bully or a victim.

As previously mentioned, this South African philosophy of unity, dignity, and respect for everyone involved in conflict puts the wrongdoer in the center of a circle of peers. For two days they tell the wrongdoer of the good they've witnessed in the wrongdoer. This brings out the innate goodness in the wrongdoer. In North America, this aligns with restorative justice and has been proven to aid the wrongdoer in restoring the damage they've caused. Restorative justice has been proven to reduce bullying and violence, and at the same time increase the wrongdoer's ability to take responsibility and make their wrongdoing right.

We don't need to do this for two days in a circle for the strategy to be effective—two minutes, done regularly, can help.

BullyProof Strategy
Insecurity is Ego

Confidence is silent. Insecurities are loud.
-Kushandwizdom

The bully needs us to feel insecure, or 'less than'.

We all know that arrogance is egotistical but did you ever consider that insecurity is also ego?

Exercise:

Sit quietly and contemplate this:

When I feel insecure, 'less than' or not good enough, that's my ego talking and me believing it. Is that who I am?

Feel this: "When I feel insecurity, it's my ego."

BullyProof Strategy
Digging Up Insecurities – What I Believe I Lack

I have not failed.
I've just found 10,000 ways that won't work.
-Thomas A. Edison

When we are secure, we can't be pushed around so easily.

One cure for the other bullying us is to see where our insecurities are
and dissolve them because they don't serve us and are disrespectful to
what created us. To do this we find out what it is we believe we lack
because what we think we lack causes us to feel insecure.

Exercise:

1. Think of a bully in your life.
2. With your eyes closed, ask yourself, "What do I believe I lack
   in their eyes?"
3. Wait quietly for the answer to arise. Don't 'think' it.
4. Sit quietly with what you discover and feel the feelings that arise
   until they dissipate.

Example:

1. Think of a bully in your life.
   My former friend.
2. With your eyes closed, ask yourself, "What do I believe I lack
   in their eyes?"
3. Wait quietly for the answer.
   Example answer: *I lack beauty.*
4. Sit quietly with what you discover ('I lack beauty') and feel the
   feelings that arise until they dissipate.
5. Realize that the belief 'I lack beauty' is a thought with
   feelings—they are words with sounds. *It is not a truth.* Anything

we are insecure about makes us available for others to push that button.

6. Turn the statement around to its opposite to uncover the truth and dissolve the target on your back and the stress caused by the belief.
   a. 'I lack beauty' becomes, 'I have beauty'
   b. Find 3 ways that statement is true.
      i. I'm kind and that's beautiful.
      ii. When I look at little kids, I feel beauty inside of me so I have beauty then.
      iii. I feel beauty inside of me when I smile, so I have beauty.

Now do two examples that are true for you.

1. Think of a bully in your life.
2. With your eyes closed, ask yourself, "What do I believe I lack in their eyes?"
3. Wait quietly for the answer to arise. Don't 'think' it. Wait and you will know when the right answer comes up into your awareness.
4. Sit quietly with what you discover and feel the feelings that arise until they dissipate.
5. Realize that the belief "I lack_____ " (insert what you discovered) is not a truth. Prove that to yourself with the next step.
6. Turn the statement around to its opposite and find three ways that statement is true or truer.

   I lack_____
   Becomes
   I have _____

How is that true?

1. _____

2. _____

3. _____

Repeat the exercise using another example of what you think the bully thinks you lack.

After doing this exercise a couple of times, think about the bully. *If you feel they think you lack anything else, do the exercise again on that.*

BullyProof Strategy
Insecurity Gives Me Freedom

I found one day in school a boy of medium size ill-treating a smaller boy.
I expostulated, but he replied: "The bigs hit me, so I hit the babies; that's
fair." In these words he epitomized the history of the human race.
-Bertrand Russell

Exercise:

Sit with this question:

1. "What happens that's good when I'm insecure?"
2. Sit quietly with your eyes closed and wait for something that is good (a positive word or image).

You may come up with ideas like this:

- People leave me alone.
- People don't expect much of me, so I don't have to be in the spotlight.
- People ignore me and then I'm able to do what I want.

What comes up for you?

Let's really look at what that means to you in your life. When we apply logic to our illogical ideas, we can see the ridiculousness of them and they dissolve *because we've become aware of them and they are not truths. The truth can't dissolve. Beliefs that aren't true can.*

Using the example, 'People ignore me and then I can do what I want'—means: TO GET TO DO WHAT I WANT I HAVE TO FEEL INSECURE BY UNCONSCIOUSLY WANTING PEOPLE TO IGNORE ME.

It doesn't make sense. Notice that it's a painful formula. Feel all the feelings that arise with this realization and then ponder this:

Might I be able to do what I want without this extra and painful step of needing to be insecure first.

Insecurity doesn't serve—we don't need it anymore.

BullyProof Strategy
Does Acting Insecure Help Me? Do
I Look Good? Feel Natural?

I stood up to a bully publicly and named everything
they had done. I was just lucky that it worked.
They smartened up after that.
-Anonymous

Think of someone who acts in an insecure way. Does that make them happier, a better person, successful? Do they look sensible or good in your eyes? Are you attracted to them?

That's us when we're insecure.

Insecurity isn't attractive. Conversely, security, to the point of arrogance, isn't attractive. What is attractive? Being genuine and natural.

You will notice that when you honestly ask these questions of yourself, your perspective of yourself shifts.

BullyProof Strategy
Insecurity is Disrespectful

I was shaking when I stood up to the bully. I shook for a
while after. But I did it and it shut the bully up.
-Anonymous

Ask this simple question: "Is it respectful to whatever created me to feel insecure?" While this was mentioned earlier in another strategy, it's worthy of its own contemplation.

If we came with instructions on our day of birth, it wouldn't say: Be insecure.

BullyProof Strategy
Bullying Is a "Durable Behavioral Style"

I don't know why I bullied him. I hate it now that I know what I did to him. I hate myself for doing it. Don't bully other people. It's not worth it.
-Anonymous

Psychology Today suggests that "bullying is a distinctive pattern of deliberately harming and humiliating others. It's a very durable behavioral style, largely because bullies get what they want"—at least at first.

They suggest: that bullying behavior is on the rise because children increasingly grow up without the kinds of experiences that lead to the development of social skills. It has been well-documented that free play is on the decline, but it is in playing with peers, without adult monitoring, that children develop the skills that make them well-liked by "age mates" and when they learn how to solve social problems.

Source:

Psychology Today, Bullying. Accessed August 18, 2021. https://www.psychologytoday.com/basics/bullying

By intervening with these strategies, we are breaking the 'durable style' of bullying.

BullyProof Strategy
Fear Busters (Because Fear Attracts Bullies)

*Courage doesn't always roar. Sometimes courage is the quiet voice
at the end of the day saying, "I will try again tomorrow."*
-Mary Anne Radmacher

This is a deceptively simple exercise that can help you dissolve the kind of fear that attracts bullies.

Bullies couldn't exist without victims, and they don't pick on just anyone; those singled out lack assertiveness and radiate fear long before they ever encounter a bully. No one likes a bully, but no one likes a victim either. When we're honest about it, initially we feel compassion for a victim, but eventually, if they continue on the victim path, we don't want to be around them.

The fear (when there is nothing to be afraid of) is guaranteed to dissipate if you are able to feel it fully. It has no choice but to disappear because the fear itself is not real. How you can prove this to yourself is to notice that when you feel fear and look around and see that if you're actually safe—the fear is fake fear.

It's hard to imagine that we could overcome some of our fears—maybe many of them! When we do this work, slowly, over time, fear doesn't surface when there's nothing wrong. That makes sense, yes? Fear doesn't need to arise when there is nothing to fear in the moment.

There are other mechanisms in us, like our connection to pure intelligence that are pre-wired inside of us that can help keep us safe. These mechanisms are innate and when we feel really clear, we jump straight to right action without fear. We can *believe* that fear will keep us safe, but does it? Might we be able to take action to protect ourselves or others without fear as the inspiration?

We are all scared of what looks like an unstoppable bully but being fearful as a strategy hasn't and won't help.

If you were bullied in any way when you were little, you likely experienced a lot of fear.

Is it necessary to live with it now? We're not little anymore.

As we grew up, we projected that fear onto other people (men, women, homeless people), situations (being in public, public speaking), things (heights, flying), or animals (snakes, spiders, dogs).

Even though I had big dogs growing up and as an adult, and felt no fear around them, one day years later, I began noticing I was scared of them and when *they* noticed, they would run up to me and bark. They found someone to dominate! Me. My fear brought out their instinct to dominate. With others, they didn't act like that. Little kids would run up to dogs the same size as them and the dog would lick them and roll over for a belly rub. My husband would use a commanding voice when they were near, and they'd sit down. Then I'd come along and the dog would draw upon that part of their nature that I was attracting—the aggressor to play out against my submissive fear.

Remember that fear inside of you is one thing that attracts bullies, so riding ourselves of fear also uninvites bullies into our world!

During the exercise, you may feel slight aches, pains, pressure, heat or tingling in the body. That is an indication that the fear you've unconsciously stored in the body is leaving, and sometimes, along with it, taking the troubles it was causing.

You will feel fear, possibly lots of it. Along with the fear, you will feel emotions and maybe dark thoughts. Keep feeling. The sensations and thoughts will dissipate.

Caution: If you experience extreme phobias or anaphylactic shock from anything, skip this exercise.

Exercise:

1. Make a list of things you are afraid of or use this list and add to or alter it.
2. Sit quietly with your eyes closed and feel all the feelings, emotions and physical sensations that arise with each concept until they dissipate.
3. Repeat the exercise a few times, noticing which words carry fearful feelings with them and repeat the daily or regularly until you notice the fear has abated or disappeared.

Notice how the fear reduces every time you do the exercise.

Caution: Do not do this exercise if you experience extreme phobias or anaphylactic shock from anything.

Examples of things that can cause fear:

- Conflict
- Saying 'no'
- Disapproval
- Asking questions in a public situation
- Flying
- Heights
- The dark
- Driving
- Other drivers
- Public speaking
- Pain
- Dentists
- Needles
- Doctors
- Germs
- Disease
- Disability
- Cancer
- Choking

The little book of peaceful power.

- Snakes
- Spiders
- Dogs
- Insects
- Bees
- Reptiles
- Bulls
- Sharks
- Thunderstorms
- Crowds
- Being touched
- Change
- Abandonment
- Rejection
- Being judged or criticized
- Being alone
- Death
- Fire
- Water
- Criminals
- Addicts
- The homeless
- Men
- Women
- Handicapped people
- Being attacked
- Being bullied
- Nuts or other foods. **Caution: Do not do this exercise if you experience extreme phobias or anaphylactic shock.**
- Failure
- Being shamed, humiliated or embarrassed

Add your fears and work them.

BullyProof Strategy
Liberate Yourself From Bullies
by Guy Finley

"When a resolute young fellow steps up to the great bully - the world—and takes him boldly by the beard, he is often surprised to find it comes off in his hand, and that it was only tied on to scare away the timid adventurers."
- Ralph Waldo Emerson

Guy Finley explains what it takes to liberate ourselves from any fear that wants to pull us down into its world.

For an interior bully to remain in charge of our lives, it requires us consenting to its authority.

Exercise:

Say to yourself, while sitting quietly, "I am not going to agree with you any longer." This is directed at our own inner bully.

Guy teaches that will attract to us the kind of higher strength that we need. That means our True Nature has space to appear. It's the negation of the power of the lower nature.

Bull Proof Strategy
Be Social or Be Quiet

Be kind whenever possible.
It's always possible.
-The 14th Dalai Lama

Even though your Natural Self or True Nature knows how to respond in any situation to any kind of human encounter, most of us need a little help until we've arrived back at our True Nature.

If you have some social skills, you're less likely to become a victim.

Ideas for developing social skills:

1. Notice where you have 'attitude' and replace it with a little gratitude for what you have. This helps you stay in a more positive mindset.
2. Use manners. Nobody is important enough to not use manners.
3. Don't interrupt. You are not more important than the person you are interrupting.
4. Do your share of what needs to be done wherever it needs to be done. This builds confidence and dissolves insecurity.
5. Give as generously as you can.
6. Be honest.
7. Stop complaining as a conversation tool.
8. Be genuinely yourself; don't pretend to be something you are not (when you're not genuine, you're pushing a bully's buttons).
9. Say "I don't know" when you don't.
10. Learn about the world you live in; you will be able to relate to, and converse with others in a more meaningful way.
11. Be willing to learn from others. Everyone is our teacher if we are humble enough to notice that.
12. Show appreciation to others—we couldn't exist without others.

13. Don't flatter others—ever. It's false, recognizable and off-putting. Instead, genuinely appreciate other people. Find something to like about them.

The next 7 strategies are adapted and revised for *BullyProof* from the book *Blessing Mistakes*. If you've read *Blessing Mistakes*, you are invited to do these exercises again because the more you do them, the more you release.

BullyProof Strategy
Unfriending Anger

For every minute you remain angry,
you give up sixty seconds of peace of mind.
-Ralph Waldo Emerson

We all have some anger stored in us. How we know that is that every now and then it rises up in us. Every time you do these exercises, you dissolve more anger. If all of your anger has disappeared, you don't need to read this section.

We don't need anger anymore.

Exercise

Notice the Anger

Think of a situation where someone got angry at you and began to bully you. Get an image of them in your mind's eye.

- Notice they are convinced they are right—while acting (a bit or a lot) insane.
- Notice they want what they want when they want it. (The 'I-ness in their highness is present—please bow, everyone!).
- Notice they think they are establishing authority while appearing deranged.
- Notice their threatening voice and stance—that's their strength.
- Notice they think they are intelligent (in the moment they are ranting, raving and raging).
- Notice they think it will resolve the situation, bring solution, and therefore bring about peace and calmness—that's like saying anger will ultimately lead to soothing.
- Notice they think getting angry and getting upset gets things done.

- Notice they think they have the right to bully others (they are entitled to get angry at others but no one is entitled to get angry at them).
- Notice how arrogant they are.
- Notice that they are the 'judge, jury and executioner'.
- Notice how they think they are exerting control by losing their own control.
- Notice how powerful they think they are.
- Notice how upset they are acting.
- Notice how much pain they are causing themselves.
- Notice how ridiculous they look.
- Notice they think they are special and should get what they want and when they don't, they get mad.
- Notice that they think they are reasonable but are really just waring.
- Notice they are a bag of wind.
- Notice an angry person, or a bully, thinks they are coming from a mentally superior position when they are really coming from a mentally inferior position.

Notice that's us when we are angry and being a bully.

This exercise invites you to get very clear about how you present when you're angry.

Ask yourself this question, "Do I want to continue to live in anger?"

BullyProof Strategy
Anger's True Signature

*"To me, habitual anger is like
sitting in a corner with a dunce cap on."*
-Louise Hay

*"That visual alone could have a discouraging effect.
Thank you, Louise."*
-Lesia (my inner work buddy)

Exercise:

When you're bullying yourself or another person imagine you have a dunce cap on your head. That might stop you. Better yet, get a dunce cap and go stick it on your head every time you feel anger.

PLEASE NOTICE THAT EVERY SINGLE TIME YOU GET ANGRY AND BULLY SOMEONE, YOU WILL THINK LIKE A DUNCE, SPEAK LIKE A DUNCE AND ACT LIKE A DUNCE.

BullyProof Strategy
Pondering Anger

Try to find one good reason to be angry. I haven't found one. I'm still looking. Wellbeing can't be found near anger. Get weary enough of the anger to be willing to do the exercises to exorcise it.

Is it okay with you to be taken over by anger? If we don't dissolve the anger, we are agreeing to it and saying it's okay to continue bullying ourselves and others.

Anger is hatred. Anger puts our bodies, our relationships and our wellbeing at risk. Polishing our anger shrivels our hearts. Anger hemorrhages our energy.

Gratitude is the opposite of anger. Anger shuts down our immune system. Gratitude improves it by 50% according to Dr. Joe Dispenza.

If we dissolve our anger, what's left IS gratitude.

Dr. Joe, who has studied and recorded his work with brain scans says that we are in a stressed state 70% of the time. Anger is a stressed state. Getting rid of it gets rid of a lot of stress.

Become discontent with anger.

Become discontent with your inner bully.

Become discontent with bullies in the world.

Become discontent with your angry inner victim.

The little book of peaceful power.

Exercise:

Sit in contemplation with this question (for several minutes):

"Is anger helpful to me?"

Something peaceful exists before anger. Contemplation can help you find that.

BullyProof Strategy
The 'Breaking Up' Message

Violence is the last refuge of the incompetent.
-Isaac Asimov

If there is no good reason to hold onto or call upon anger, you can use one or a combination of these strategies when anger arises.

Exercise

1. Don't judge yourself when you get angry and have bullied someone. That hasn't worked and won't work.

2. Remove yourself from others before you react when you're conscious enough to do that. Don't be too hard on yourself if you can't do it all the time. Be happy if you can do it a few times. Practice helps. You'll notice that you will be so much happier with yourself when you don't involve others in your anger.

3. As John de Ruiter, a Canadian spiritual teacher suggests, keep a note in your pocket that says, "I don't need my raging story anymore," and pull it out and read it every time anger arises.

   a. To rid yourself of your inner victim, keep a note in your pocket and every time you notice the feeling of victimhood, pull it out and read it. "I don't need my victimhood story anymore."

   b. Do the same when you're about to bully yourself or others. "I don't need my bully story anymore."

4. Do your own inner work on the issue catalyzing the anger, using the other methods offered, such as What Do I Gain.

5. Use Ho'oponopono when anger arises (I'm sorry, please forgive me, thank you, I love you). This simple, ancient healing technique clears out energy that's damaging to us and has more than a few miracles credited to it, including a Dr. Len who

used it to cure over twenty patients in an insane asylum. Keep repeating it on any angry state until you feel release.

6. Silently step back from the anger that's accompanying the bullying behavior, watch it, and feel what it brings up.

7. Remind yourself that this angry bullying won't get you what you want: peace, connection, compassion, real solutions, etc.

8. Remind yourself you are about to, as Eckhart Tolle teaches:
   a. Get confused/unclear.
   b. Become irrational.

9. Look at an angry bully's face. Remind yourself that's what you look like when you're angry. Go look in the mirror when you're angry.

10. Remind yourself of what Sadhguru teaches, getting angry is:
    a. Truly 'mad', 'insane'.
    b. Like taking poison and expecting the other person to hurt. Remind yourself getting angry causes damaging chemical reactions in the body. We're poisoning ourselves with our anger.

11. See if you can revert your attention and fully focus on following your breath in and out for a few minutes. As taught by Eckhart Tolle, we can't think and follow our breath at the same time.

12. Apologize to others. Explain that you are working on your anger and bullying issues and can see how damaging to relationships and useless it is.

BullyProof Strategy
Dissolve Stored Up Anger

*Speak when you're angry and you'll make
the speech you'll ever regret.*
-Groucho Marx

For a proactive release of anger:

Exercise:

o   Read the first word on the list below.
o   Close your eyes after you read the word.
o   Let the word bring up any uncomfortable feelings, images, or physical sensations that it does.
o   Don't think it, feel it—if you have trouble and the mind wants to chatter, and you can't feel it:
    1. Invite yourself to focus on feeling it. It is possible to feel anything here: physical, emotional, or mental pain or discomfort (which is caused by being attached to/identified with the word you are working on). You might feel a slight pain in any area of your body, a tightening in the body, or anything at all. More than one emotion might arise. Feel any that do. A few different images might arise of past traumas, or images of future imagined traumas.
    2. If you still can't 'feel' the feelings the word brings up, think of the feeling of the sun on your face and feel that, and then switch back to feeling the uncomfortable word. Remind yourself, you are doing this to free yourself of anger because it's not a natural part of you.
-   Remind yourself of the word you're working on if you lose focus and then sink into focusing on inside of yourself (for example, inside of your throat and then broaden it to include the whole of the inside of you).

- Say to yourself, while you feel it, "I'm so sorry I'm attached to (insert the word you are working with)."
- Feel it until it lets go—you will feel a softening once the concept has been released and the sensations that were present during the process will disappear.
- This releases whatever you are able to let go of at this time. There may be more that you can release another time.
- We build layers over time and that's one reason the same emotion or issue comes up repeatedly for releasing. As we go through more layers, we find that we are operating more from our naturally joyful and harmless states.
- Do as many words as you want in one sitting (remembering to do each word separately) and then come back to the list until you've gone through it completely.
- Each word may need to be felt for different lengths of time. It usually only takes a minute or two but could take more or less time.
- Some words will feel stronger and more painful than others.
- If the image of another person arises while you are doing this, bring your attention back to inside of yourself and keep feeling what this feels like inside of you. Clearing this in you can help clear it in others, but that's not the goal. If it doesn't clear it in others, at least we can be more peaceful when faced with their anger. The goal is to free ourselves of our anger and bring us back to feeling true inner wellbeing.
- After you've done the list once, do it again. The more you do it, the more you release.
- After the inner work is done, Bless your Mistake for reverting to anger as an old ingrained, programmed habit, "I matter more the mistake of being an angry victim/angry bully," and make it right to anyone you need to.
- If you like, you can say, "Goodbye _____, I don't need you anymore."

Abrupt, Admonishing, Affronted, Aflame, Aggravated, Aggressive, Angry, Annoyed, Antagonistic, Apoplectic, Argumentative, Awful, Bad-tempered, Badgering, Belligerent, Beside myself, Blazing,

Blistering, Blustering, Bothered, Boiling, Brusque, Brutal, **Bullying**, Burning, Cantankerous, Castigating, Caustic, Censuring, Chastising, Cheesed off, Cold, Complaining, Confrontational, Contentious, Crabby, Cranky, Critical, Cross, Cruel, Curt, Dangerous, Defensive, Defiant, Demanding, Difficult, Disapproving, Disciplining, Discontent, Disgruntled, Displeased, Disrespectful, Dissatisfied, Disturbed, Edgy, Enraged, Exasperated, Exasperating, Explosive, Fanatical, Ferocious, Fiery, Foul, Fractious, Frenzied, Frothing, Fuming, Furious, Gnashing, Goading, Getting on my nerves, Grouchy, Grumpy, Gunning (for someone), Harassing, Harsh, Hassling, Hateful, Heated, Hopping mad, Hostile, Hot-headed, Hounding, Huffy, Impatient, Impudent, Incensed, Inciting, Indignant, Infuriated, Insane (the angry kind), Insistent, Insolent, Insulting, Intolerant, Ire, Irking, Irritable, Irritated, Justifying, Livid, Mad, Moody, Nagging, Narrow-minded, Objecting, Offended, Offensive, Opinionated, Ornery, Out of sorts, Outraged, Passive-aggressive, Peevish, Penalizing, Petulant, Picky, Piqued, Prejudiced, Prickly, Provoked, Provoking, Pugnacious, Punishing, Punitive, Pushy, Put out, Quarrelsome, Rabid, Raging, Reactive, Rebuking, Rejecting, Relentless, Reprimanding, Reproving, Resentful, Rigid, Riled, Rude, Ruthless, Sadistic, Scalding, Scorching, Searing, Seething, Severe, Sharp, Short-tempered, Slighting, Smoldering, Snappy, Snippy, Spitting mad, Special (we get mad when someone doesn't treat us a special), Spoiling (for a fight), Stern, Stinging, Strict, Stubborn, Surly, Teed off, Temper Tantrumer, Terrible, Terse, Testy, Threatening, Ticked off, Touchy, Truculent, Uncompromising, Unrelenting, Up in arms, Vehement, Vexed, Vexing, Violent, **Violent Victim**, **Victim**, **Submissive Victim**, Witch-hunter, Worked up, Wound up, Wrathful.

It's hard to do this whole list. The mind doesn't want to. The heart does. Bookmark the page and keep it on your nightstand, doing a few before bed each night until you've gone through the list and the anger runs out of you in rivers. Before you go to sleep, utter a prayer of gratitude for the peace you feel after releasing anger.

BullyProof Strategy
Resentment & Bitterness

There are no justified resentments
-Dr. Wayne Dyer

Notice who is hurting when *you* hold resentment and bitterness about the past and those who bullied you. Holding onto resentment is against our own wellbeing. Staying in a bitter state can't be good for us.

And how can it be true that there are no justified resentments? Because hurting myself over what someone else did or said *is not justified*.

Exercise:

Sit quietly and feel into each of these questions until you feel some release from a new understanding or perspective:

-   Do I want to feel resentment and bitterness?
-   Is there a good reason (even one good reason) for me to feel resentment and bitterness?
-   Will it help me in any way (if I feel resentment and bitterness)?
-   Is feeling resentment and bitterness relevant in this moment?
-   Could I send love to that person who bullied me, so I can feel the feeling of love inside of me instead of hate? (The Prayer of St. Francis: "Where there is hatred, let me sow love"). Do this for your own sake.
-   Could I Bless myself for this mistake of harboring resentment and bitterness? Say and feel the truth of this statement: "I matter so much more than this mistake of hurting myself by staying resentful and bitter."
-   Could I Bless others for their mistakes? "_____ (name of the person who bullied you), you matter so much more as a human being than your mistake does. I know you suffered

when you made the mistake because I know I suffer when I make one."

- Could I Bless myself for hurting others and making them feel resentment and bitterness? "I matter so much more than the mistake of bullying and hurting others." Then, as best as you can, make all your mistakes right—for you own wellbeing.

BullyProof Strategy
Freedom From the Trauma Trap

*One day you will tell your story of how you overcame what you
went through and it will be someone else's survival guide.*
-Unknown

Traumas are real and painful, but it's our job to make sure we don't
stay a victim for long because that invites more pain, abuse and traumas
into our lives.

This strategy is to release the painful past because the event we suffered
is not here now.

**IF YOU HAVE NO TRAUMATIC OR PAINFUL FEELINGS
FROM BEING BULLIED OR NEVER FEEL LIKE A
HELPLESS VICTIM, SKIP THIS SECTION.**

*Nothing happened in your past
that can keep you from the present.*
-Eckhart Tolle

This exercise uses self-reflection to set us free of the pain of the past,
which will reduce the urge to:

- bully ourselves
- bully another person, or
- feel and act like a helpless victim
- suffer from past events whether we were the victim or the bully

If we don't feel hurt, we don't feel like hurting another.

Once we clear the pain attached to memories of the past, *we won't
be informed by our past hurts* as a way of dealing with whatever is
happening now.

We don't need the pain of the past influencing us anymore. We can remember the event so we know what we want in our lives, or what to do in a stressful circumstance—without needing to feel the pain of the emotions attached to the past event—ever again.

We can use awareness to help inform us about how to handle challenges that come up. By listing our traumas and working through them, we leave the painful feelings around them in the past where they belong.

This exercise turns trauma into triumph instead of having to relive painful emotions from painful experiences.

List every bullying event, trauma, major upset, or crisis you ever experienced.

Do the exercise on one or two past traumas a day or more or whatever feels right for you.

Write these questions and the new awarenesses that arise from them in your journal about each incident.

- Who was there, what were they doing, what did their faces look like, what did they say and do? Include the sights and sounds and other sensory information.
- What did you say and do?
- What feelings come up now (feel them until they dissolve, which dilutes the attachment to the event and dissolves the stored-up emotions).
- How is it true that the traumatic event changed your life in a good way? What path did it send you on. Did it teach you something you wouldn't have learned otherwise? What *changed* in a good way after this incident?
- What is one good reason to hold onto the resentment?
- Who are you hurting when you relive this painful trauma?
- Does hating the perpetrator help you or hurt you?
- Is the trauma happening now other than in your mind?

- Would it be better for you to forgive them? Would forgiving them release you? Can you accept that you can't forgive them—if you can't? What would it take to forgive them for your own sake?
- What would it take to feel compassion for them, since they couldn't do any differently than they did at the time due to their conditioning and beliefs?
- Forgive yourself for not having compassion (if you don't feel compassion).
- Bless your mistake of not having compassion, which would feel better inside of you. "I matter more than this mistake of not having compassion."
- Do Ho'oponopono: repeat "I'm sorry, please forgive me, thank you, I love you," until more peace is felt.
- How do you feel after all of that? Repeat until there is release.

Example:

Trauma: he's backing away from me, spewing hatred, saying he's got a gun.

Who was there, what did they say or do: it's night, my husband, him and his wife are on the deck.

What did I say or do? froze.

What feelings come up? intense fear.

What sights, sounds, etc. come up? the adrenaline rush is all I can feel.

What images come up: years of his drunken antics—his lack of empathy and violent tendencies.

How is it true that the traumatic event changed your life in a good way? What path did it send you on. Did it teach you something you wouldn't have learned otherwise? What changed in a good way after this incident? I discovered how to use self-inquiry and in using the strategies, he disappeared from my life. I wrote this book. I gained so many insights on bullying. I stopped being a bully. I can help others because of my own experience.

What is one good reason to hold onto the resentment? I can't find one that's true.

Who are you hurting when you relive this painful trauma? Me.

Does hating the perpetrator help you or hurt you? Hurt me.

Is the trauma happening now other than in your mind? No, it's only in my mind.

Would it be better for you to forgive them? Would forgiving them release you? Can you accept that you can't forgive them, if you can't? What would it take to forgive them for your own sake? I don't feel like forgiving him or her. I know it would help me. I can accept that I can't forgive. That brings up emotional pain.

What would it take to feel compassion? Logical thinking: he was drunk and might not even remember. I know that I suffer when I do unconscious things or speak unconsciously, so he must suffer too, when he acts out. But I'm resisting feeling compassion for them.

Bless yourself for not having compassion, "I do matter more than this mistake of not having compassion for my suffering fellow human beings." Release comes and I feel compassion for all of us.

Do Ho'oponopono: repeat "I'm sorry, please forgive me, thank you, I love you," until more peace is felt.

How do you feel after all of that? Repeat until there is release. I feel peaceful at the moment and will do the exercise again if the trauma arises again.

BullyProof Strategy
Dissolving Guilt

If your compassion does not include yourself, it is incomplete.
-Jack Kornfield

Guilt—we don't need it anymore.

List the times you've inflicted pain on and caused trauma to others.

Example:

Trauma you caused another person: I made my child walk home from the store.

Who was there, what did they say or do: him and I.

What did you say or do: gave him a warning and then told him he had to walk home. He was so scared he ran all the way. We lived two miles out of town.

What feelings come up now: sadness, grief, regret.

What images come up now: seeing him run through the field towards home. Seeing him sitting on the swing outside, wondering if he should come in.

What sights, sounds, etc. come up: the fear on his face.

How is it true that the traumatic event changed your life in a good way? What path did it send you on. Did it teach you something you wouldn't have learned otherwise? What changed in a good way after this incident? I saw what I didn't want to be as a parent.

What is one good reason to hold onto the resentment? I can't find one that's true.

Who are you hurting when you relive this painful trauma? Me.

Does hating yourself as the perpetrator help you or hurt you? I'm the perpetrator and hating myself hurst me. I can feel the pain of hating myself right now.

Is the trauma happening now other than in your mind? No, it's only in my mind.

Would it be better for you to forgive yourself? Would forgiving yourself release you? Can you accept that you can't forgive yourself if you can't? What would it take to forgive yourself for your own sake? I don't feel like forgiving myself. I know it would help me.

What would it take to feel compassion for yourself? Logical thinking: this suffering is useless. It serves no purpose other than if I apply a strategy of awareness to it, I come into more awareness about what's in my unconscious mind that's causing this pain. I still don't feel compassion for myself, yet.

Bless yourself for not having compassion, "I do matter more than this mistake of not having compassion for myself." Some release comes.

Do Ho'oponopono: repeat "I'm sorry, please forgive me, thank you, I love you," until more peace is felt. I have to do this for many minutes.

How do you feel after all of that? Repeat until there is release. Relaxed. Relief. Another layer of suffering is gone.

Think of the situation again and if anything, other than peace comes up, do the inquiry again or do Ho'oponopono again until relief comes. Each time more suffering will be released until you feel love towards yourself and then you know you're free. Each time guilt tries to impose itself on you, remind yourself it's useless, painful and can be dissolved. Do any part of the exercise that will help you do that.

The little book of peaceful power.

CHAPTER 4

Teaching Kids To BullyProof Themselves

BullyProof Strategy
Teaching Kids What To Do When
Encountering A Bully Through A Story

> *There is no exercise better for the heart*
> *than reaching down and lifting people up.*
> *-John Holmes*

Excerpt from *Tuskie's Travels*
By *Brenda Miller*

Being BullyProof in Bangkok

> *...you don't have to wait for someone*
> *to treat you bad repeatedly...*
> *-Jane Green*

"What's a bully?" asked Lexi the Sloth, happily perched beside Wally the Wombat and Taloola the Owl right on top of Mr. Tuskerelephas's head. While Tuskie has a lot of nicknames, his formal name is Mr. Tuskerelephas. They were getting ready for the world's largest water fight at the Songkran festival. They were so excited. They'd never heard of a water fight having its own festival. What fun!

The little book of peaceful power.

"A bully is anyone who–" Mr. Tusker started to speak but all the animals jumped in to comment. Mr. Tuskerelephas grinned.

"A bully is somebody who pushes you—hard——a lot," stated Taloola the Owl.

"A bully is a big meanie," added Wally the Wombat.

"A bully is somebody who says really bad stuff to you," said Minnie the Hippo.

"A bully is somebody who hits you," said Sparky the Dragon, who immediately blew the word 'bully' into the sky.

"A bully is bad," said Glitter the Seahorse.

"Oh no, a bully is not bad," corrected Mr. Tuskie. "A bully just thinks they're bad, that's why they behave badly. Deep inside they are just like we are—pure goodness."

"I know how we are deep inside, even though my insides aren't very deep," cried Mr. King Cobra with no fangs. "Super-powered-peaceful."

"I know too. It feels like fun," said Happy the Dog, grinning at the idea of fun.

"What we are deep inside is a *secret secret*," said Mr. Tuskerelephas. "A most amazing one. It's kind of like a wonder. Deep inside is our true nature. That's when we feel natural. There is a feeling that nothing is wrong."

They all chimed in their perception of what felt natural.

"I feel natural when I belly laugh," announced Daisy the Pony.

"It's like how I feel when I pet my puppy," said Uni the Unicorn.

The little book of peaceful power.

"It's like how I feel when I help someone," said Mama Llama.

"It's like how I feel when I'm playing," said Hawk.

"It's like how I feel when someone holds my hand," said _____(name of your child's animal).

"It's like when I am doing crafts," said Marshmallow the Giraffe.

"It's like when I am looking at the mountains and the sky and feeling that nice feeling," said Buster Beats the DJ Gorilla.

"It's like when all of me feels quiet," said Mr. Zebra.

"It's like when someone gives me a hug when I feel bad," said Jessica the Dolphin.

"It's like when I say something kind," said Zuzu the Cow.

"It's like when I Bless my Mistake," said Mr. Bear.

"Yah, it's like when I get Blessed for my Mistake," responded Ms. Gazelle.

"AND it's how I feel inside when I Bless *your* Mistake," added Zippa the Monkey.

"It's like when I stay quiet when someone is upset," said Lexi.

"It's like when I'm in the zone," said Taloola.

"It's like when I'm nice instead of mean and really mean it!" said Wally.

"It's when I wish upon a star for everyone to feel good inside," said Doodle the Duck.

"It's how I feel when I lay down on the grass," said Stella the Phoenix.

The little book of peaceful power.

"It's how I feel when I'm in my garden," said Fluffles the Hamster.

"It's how I feel when I *feel* thank you," said Sapphire the White Siberian Tiger.

"How do you feel thank you?" asked Jessica.

"I know a fun way to find out," said Mr. Tuskie "Say it, but don't feel it."

That was easy enough, and then, as usual chaos reigned while they hollered, snorted, belted and bellered 'thank you'.

"Now feel it instead of saying it."

That brought about complete silence.

"It feels good to feel it!" announced Mama Llama.

"So, bullies are the same as us? Their true nature is the same?" asked Taloola.

"Yep, their true nature is exactly the same as our true nature," said Mr. Tuskerelephas.

"Then why does a bully act bad instead of natural?" asked Lexi.

"Because they think they're bad, so they act bad. They are trying to get rid of their badness in a way that doesn't work at all."

"I know a secret," said Mr. Tusker.

That got everyone's attention, as it always did. They all loved secrets, and all of Mr. T's secrets always made them feel better.

"There's a way to bully-proof yourself so others don't bully you, and to also take the bullying part of you right out of you!"

"Huh, I'm not a bully," said Ms. Gazelle.

"We all act like a bit of bully now and then," said Mr. Tuskerelephas.

"Even you and Sadhguru?" asked Happy the Dog.

"No, once you relax back into your true nature, you don't feel the need to bully anyone. You don't ever think about acting that way."

"I sometimes bully my little brother," said Fluffles. "It doesn't really feel good but I don't know how to stop."

"Me too," Ms. Gazelle said, looking sheepish. She was realizing that she had, indeed, acted like a bully. Not once, but many times. There was the time . . . and the time . . . and the time . . . There were actually a lot of times.

"The first thing we do to bully-proof ourselves is to close our eyes and recognize when we have been a bully, when we've hit or pushed another person, or criticized them, or let loose on them with nasty words—repeatedly," invited Mr. Tusker.

"We have to do this as well as the other strategies to make sure we've got all the bases covered," said Mr. T.

"What's that mean?" asked Ms. Gazelle.

"It means one strategy isn't enough. It takes a few of them to make a change."

In the meantime, Doodle had been pondering where he bullied someone.

"Oh," said, Doodle, "I quacked really loud at my kids—repeatedly. I'll close my eyes but I already feel how awful it feels."

"Bless you for your Mistake, Doodle," said Fluffles, who was super at recognizing and blessing mistakes.

The little book of peaceful power.

Each of the animals contributed with what they saw about themselves. It didn't feel nice but after they felt how not-nice it felt, they felt *way* better. That's because they'd learned another secret: if you 'see' it you're less likely to 'be' it! If you see and feel it, the bad feelings disappear!

"Another way to stop someone from bullying is to tell them, 'No,' when it feels safe to do that.

"No," whispered Hawk.

"Firmly," said Mr. Tuskerelephas with a kindly smile towards Hawk. "That's another secret."

"Hold your hand out and say, 'Stop. You can't bully me,'" he said.

They practised holding out their hand, hoof, claw, foot, or any other part that would do the job and said, "No." It felt good, but nobody was bullying them at the moment, either. Maybe the practise helped.

"Keep your 'calm, firm' eyes on their eyes and don't back down. Unless they are going to physically hurt you, then you go, but in your heart, you don't back down. Even if they are bigger than you, and even when you're scared. Bullies sometimes stop when they are told 'No!' because they're shocked that someone would tell them 'No.' And underneath the bullying, they are scared, too."

"They don't act like it," said Happy, and the crew agreed.

"When you get really scared, like if a dog attacks you, sorry, not you Happy, but if a big mean snarly dog attacks you with its fangs bared, you can get really scared and then in that moment, or later, get really angry and become a bully yourself. You might bully yourself or someone else. Unfortunately, we pass these things along if we don't dissolve them when then come up."

They pondered that for a little while and then agreed. That was kind of like another secret. There were so many secret secrets to learn!

The festival had begun and they all had water guns and water balloons and buckets of water. They all started playing. Even the police joined in the fun!

But there was a rat who kept pushing everyone and spraying them in the face and taking all the fun out of the good time.

Hawk, who didn't want bullies to get away with bullying, felt scared, but safe enough with all these good animals around him, to walk right up to the rat, even though his feathers were shaking, and firmly say, "No! Stop!"

The rat looked surprised and snarled, but Hawk stood his ground and the rat turned and ran away.

"I did it!" His feathers weren't the only thing shaking. He was shaking inside, too, but he didn't feel so powerless anymore.

After making sure the bully was gone, Hawk did as Mr. Uskie had taught them during one of the lessons about bullies and jumped up in the air to make a 'Hi-Ya' symbol with his feet (which worked just as well as hands anyway)!

Hawk felt the peaceful power surge through him of proclaiming 'Hi-Ya'. It means 'I'm not powerless.'

Some of the other animals, in solidarity, dawned their Superman and Superwoman headbands and capes to feel their own peaceful power!

"Fear doesn't matter if you really want something," Mr. Tuskerelephas said, noticing Hawk's feathers shaking.

That needed a bit of pondering. We might be fearful about something, but that isn't the important thing when we really want something. More fun secret secrets!

"I used to feel so defenseless against bullies. I didn't feel like there was anything I could do. Now I know there is something I can do. I felt safe enough to do it because you were all here," Hawk said. The whole crew cheered for Hawk and they all felt like maybe they might be able to do the same to a bully.

"We had a bullying experience, so we need to look again and see where we are bullies," said Mr. Tuskie. "It's helpful to do this exercise a few times and then every time we notice we're being bullied or are acting like one. It's not always enough to permanently stop a bully by saying stop."

"Wait! What?" cried Mr. King Cobra with no Fangs, "I'm not a bully."

"You know we've all acted like bullies and if we close our eyes and ask to see when or where, we'll see it."

Dead silence. Even though no one wanted to do it again—see where they were bullies, they knew Mr. Tuskie never led them wrong.

Glitter said, "I'll do it," and immediately closed her eyes, opening them a few seconds later. "I can see where I bullied Minnie when I pinched her when I got mad—a bunch of times."

Glitter hung her seahorse head and felt the feelings that revelation brought up. It was not nice.

"You matter more than your mistake, Glitter," said Mr. Tusker.

That brought Glitter's head up and she realized that was true, she did matter more than her mistake, but she also knew she had to apologize to Minnie. That even felt better than hiding her mistake of bullying.

The whole crew joined in to see and then free themselves of acting like bullies. There were a few tears but, in the end, everyone felt better. As usual when they did one of Mr. Usker's joy-tools.

"We bully ourselves too," said Mr. Tuskerelephas.

"What, how?" asked Happy the Dog.

"When we say to ourselves, 'I'm ugly', 'I'm bad.' Those are some of the ways we bully ourselves."

They took a minute to realize that was true. And silly.

It doesn't make sense to bully ourselves, we're supposed to be on our own team.

"Yes, so to stop that, we have to notice every time we bully ourselves and tell ourselves, 'That bully in me is not how I feel best,'" said Mr. Elephas.

"Another way to say that," cried Hawk, "Is—you're not the boss of me!" He flapped his wings in joyful confirmation!

"Will that stop it?" asked Mama Llama.

"Yes, over time, it will. You will begin to notice what wellbeing is and you will want to give it to yourself," said Mr. Tuskerelephas.

"I'm a bigger bully than I thought," said Ms. Gazelle, shrinking as small as she could.

Mr. Tusker hugged Ms. Gazelle and asked her to stand in the middle while the animals made a circle around her.

She started crying big gazelle tears. "I hurt my kids when I bully them with criticism and judgment and a know-it-all attitude. I feel awful."

The little book of peaceful power.

Mr. Tuskerelephas, said, "Ms. Gazelle, you don't feel good when you bully someone, and right now you are bullying yourself."

She cried harder.

"You can help yourself, Ms. Gazelle," said Mr. T.

He invited each animal to do what they learned in South Africa: Ubuntu, which means give humanity to others. It was to show Ms. Gazelle that even though she'd made the mistake of bullying, she was still a good person inside, and that her true nature also shone through her a lot of times.

"I love that you are always so inspired when you do anything," Mr. Tuskie said.

She looked up and her tears slowed. But she didn't feel like she deserved this kindness.

The other animals joined in.

"I love that you are generous!" said Glitter the Seahorse.

"I think you're really good at whatever you do," said Mr. King Cobra with no fangs.

"I often see you helping one of us," said Sparky and breathed the word 'help' into the sky.

"I love it when you belly-laugh," Minnie the Hippo said.

Ms. Gazelle's tears dried up. "You do?" she asked.

"Yes, a lot."

"Remember the time I knocked over the Eiffel Tower in Paris and you said, "It's okay, Mr. Tuskie, we'll find a way to fix it,'" said Mr. Tuskerelephas.

"Yes," sniffled Ms. Gazelle.

"That was really nice of you because that was a really big mistake I made," said Mr. Tusker.

A smile started to form on Ms. Gazelle's face.

"And remember the time you helped that hungry rabbit? That was really great of you," said Mama Llama.

"And you love easily," said Buster Beats the DJ Gorilla.

The crew went on, 'flooding love' all over Ms. Gazelle until she was filled up with it.

"It's true that I don't feel good when I'm being a bully, but I sure feel good now," said Ms. Gazelle. "That must mean bullying isn't good for me. Thank you," she added and beamed at the crew. "I don't feel like bullying anymore now. I feel like loving everyone and helping as much as I can." She thought to herself, *That must be good for me.*

"Love," said Mr. Tuskie, "is the opposite of bullying."

"What happens when you bully someone?" asked Mr. Bear.

"Consequences are attached to all actions, as we know," said Mr. Tuskerelephas. "See how bad Ms. Gazelle felt. That's a consequence of bullying. You might not notice, but you'll feel bad in the moment and for a long time after, you will think about it and feel bad."

"I know, I know, I know," said _____(name of your child's animal), "Bullies don't have lots of friends."

"That's right! The other animals don't want to play with me if I'm mean to them or bully them," said Doodle the Duck.

"I get madder and madder if I bully someone. It doesn't help me," said Daisy the Pony.

"It's no fun to be a bully or to be around one," said Taloola.

"A bully has no bliss," said Bruce.

"And I get mad and scared when somebody bullies me," said King Cobra with no fangs. "I just want to slither away—fast!"

"I have a question," said Ms. Gazelle. "Why do the other animals pick on me?" she asked Mr. Tuskerelephas.

"Because, as another wise man teaches, 'The bully is insecure and the victim is insecure.' The cure for bullying and being bullied is the same: lots and lots of real love."

"Does everyone know about this?" asked Marshmallow the Giraffe. "It seems important."

"Not too many people know this, that's why it's called a *secret secret*, but now you know it, and you can share it with others and maybe eventually everyone can stop bullying, since it does no good anyway."

"I know another secret," said Mr. Tuskerelephas. "You must always make sure you tell a responsible adult if you are being bullied. No matter what the bully says. That's called 'sharing our dragons' and it makes us feel better right away. There is a proverb that goes like this: 'A problem shared is a problem halved.'"

"What's that mean?" asked Zuzu the Cow.

"It means when we tell our troubles to someone, especially if they have some wisdom about life, we don't feel as upset or burdened by the problem. And when we're not so upset, we can think more clearly about what to do about a bully," said Mr. T. It doesn't always make things right, but it can make them better.

The little book of peaceful power.

"Another *secret secret* I know about this bullying business is that we need to forgive them and one of the best ways to do that is to Bless them like we do when someone makes a mistake. Bullying is a mistake, and Blessing their Mistake is also for your own wellbeing. You feel better inside when you give someone Grace instead of grief when they make a mistake. They are good deep inside of themselves, and they matter so much more than the mistake they are making of bullying others. You don't want to say it out loud to them, or you may, but for sure, say it in your mind to them, 'You matter more than the mistake does.' This will make you feel good inside too, and that's one thing we all love!"

"But," added Mr. T, it's important to remember that you don't bless their mistake out loud unless they feel bad and admitted to it—if they haven't, you saying it will cause more trouble.

Feeling better, once again, they rejoined the water fight!

But the rat came back! It started spewing ugly words at the crew. Mr. Tuskerelephas said, "I know another secret!"

The animals held their tongues and didn't lash back at the rat; they waited because Mr. Tuskie never let them down. They knew he would handle this little bully and they'd learn something, too.

Mr. Tuskie smiled at the rat then turned to the crew and said, "The Buddha taught that if someone gives you a gift in the way of their anger or upset behaviour, if you don't accept it, who does the gift belong to?"

The crew caught what he taught: don't react, and rather, realize the other's behaviour is theirs. You don't accept their anger even if they want to give it to you.

He just kept smiling at the rat. The rat didn't know what to do. He was rude, mean, and plain old nasty, and Mr. Tusker Tuskie continued to smile in a kindly way at him. The rat finally ran out of anger and said, "Why aren't you scared of me?"

"Because I'm happy inside of myself, so I don't accept your anger. I want to stay feeling happy."

The rat didn't know what to make of that, but he could see that he couldn't bait anyone here, so he ran off again.

It was so good for the crew to see that. Bullies don't always win!

"There's one last thing. When someone bullies you with words, remember this: Don't believe the bully!"

That brought on the usual cacophony with all the animals hollering, "Don't believe the bully! They don't make any sense."

"They say things like, 'You should never have been born.' Is a bully in charge of who should be born?"

Well, that was interesting to think about. Of course, a bully isn't in charge of who should be born.

After the water fun they went shopping.

When an angry shopkeeper chased them out of one shop, they decided to leave peacefully and a little more quickly, because the shopkeeper had a stick! They didn't know what they had done because they couldn't understand the local language, but they understood the stick, so they just skedaddled!

"I wonder if he's a bully," pondered Hawk.

"I think so. Bless him," Mama Llama said while in full flight.

Sometimes it's best to run!

The End.

Lessons and Exercises

I am That: When I See It, I No Longer Be It!

1. When you encounter a bully, and when you are in a safe place, close your eyes, get quiet, and ask to be shown a time when you behaved like a bully to someone else.
2. Acknowledge what it feels like to behave like a bully towards another person.
3. Notice times when you bully yourself and acknowledge what that feels like.
4. Feel all the feelings that come up until they naturally disappear, taking the bad feelings with them.

That's Not I

- Teach your children that when they feel natural, they are in their nature.
- When they don't feel natural, invite them to notice that they are in an upset or negative state and that if they see 'That's not I,' the upset will let go of them.

Saying No

- When it feels and seems right and safe to do so, tell the bully, "No" or "Stop." Hold out your hand in the traditional stop sign if it feels okay for you to do that.

The Love Flooding Method as taught by Susan Stiffleman

- To instill security in your child whether they are a bully or a victim, since both are insecure, make a list of ten things you truly love about them, and then, in private, tell them.
- The security they feel will help them refrain from bullying themselves, and, at the same time, release the energy of insecurity in them that attracts a bully.

The little book of peaceful power.

Perform a Version of Ubuntu

- When your child is a bully, invite everyone involved to tell them all the good things about them.
- When your child is a victim, do the same.

Blessing Mistakes

- As learned in the lesson on Blessing Mistakes, when your child bullies, say to them, "You matter more than the mistake of bullying (or acting out in that way)." Teach your child that they will feel better if they make their mistake right than if they deny, hide, or justify it.

Buddha: Don't Accept The Gift

- If you are able to stand quietly while someone says nasty things and refuse the 'gift' they are trying to give you, as the Buddha taught, the gift belongs to the one giving it.
- Let the other keep their anger, and you keep your peace.

Sharing our Dragons, Our Troubled Thoughts, and Experiences

- The proverb, 'Troubles shared are troubles halved," will encourage kids to share their troubles, especially if you listen carefully, take care to not overreact, do your own work if you do, and help them do their own work on the issue.

The Bully is Insecure and The Victim is Insecure as taught by Eckhart Tolle and Dr. Shefali

- Understanding this statement will make *you* more understanding towards bullies and their victims.
- Find ways, including the strategies in the book, to help others come back into their nature where they naturally feel secure.

Buy A Superman or Superwoman headband and/or cape and use it during role playing with your child. Practice the Superman and Superwoman stance along with 'Hi-Ya!'

CHAPTER 5

Get Help

The ones that are crazy enough to think they can
change the world are the ones that do.
-Steve Jobs

Education on The Prevention of Harm

kidpower International is an organization that specializes in personal safety education for all ages. https://www.kidpower.org

Bullying and Suicide

The CDC reports 4,400 deaths per year to suicide. 14% of students have considered it.

Half of suicides in Britain are caused by bullying.

Source: *Bullying and Suicide*
Accessed November 30, 2021. http://www.bullyingstatistics.org/content/bullying-and-suicide.html

If bullying means you, or someone you know, feels suicidal, please call:

For International Suicide Hotlines:
https://www.opencounseling.com/suicide-hotlines

In Canada:
Canadian Suicide Prevention Service
833-456-4566

In the United States:
www.suicide.org to find a helpline.

USA National Suicide Prevention Life Line **911 (after July 16, 2022) DIAL 988.** Find the fact sheet here:
https://www.fcc.gov/sites/default/files/988-fact-sheet.pdf

There are many organizations that can help. This list is from: www.helpguide.org

www.bullyingcanada.ca
www.stopbullying.gov
www.pacer.org
Dealing with Bullying – Help for teenagers in dealing with bullies and bullying. (TeensHealth)
It Gets Better – Videos for LGBT kids and teens. (It Gets Better Project)
Resilience Guide for Parents and Teachers – Building resilience in children. (APA)
Bullying Prevention and Intervention – Tips on prevention and intervention for school administrators, teachers, family members, and students. (ADL)
Teaching Kids Not to Bully – How to help kids stop bullying. (KidsHealth)
Bullying helplines:
U.S.: 1-800-273-8255 – Crisis Call Center
UK: 0845 22 55 787 – National Bullying Helpline
Canada: 1-877-352-4497 – BullyingCanada
Australia:1800 551 800 – Kids Helpline
New Zealand: 0800 54 37 54 – Kidsline
Help for gay and lesbian youths being bullied:
U.S.: 1-866-488-7386 – The Trevor Project
UK: 0800 999 5428 – Galop
Canada: PFLAG Canada offers regional numbers
Australia: 1800 184 527 – Qlife

The End (of great amounts of bullying).

You are invited to take the course on Bullying on <u>www. thekidcode.ca</u> It will help.

xoBrenda

Printed in the United States
by Baker & Taylor Publisher Services